OUT OF
THE FLAMES

*The Story of the Fire Services National
Benevolent Fund 1943-2003*

OUT OF THE FLAMES

The Story of the Fire Services National Benevolent Fund 1943-2003

Neil Wallington

FSNBF

FIRE SERVICES NATIONAL BENEVOLENT FUND

DEDICATION

This book is dedicated jointly to all the many men and women of the British Fire Service who, in both war and peacetime, have sacrificed their lives or been seriously injured in protecting their fellow beings from the ravages of fire, and to all those who have been involved with the Fire Services National Benevolent Fund and its work over the past 60 years.

Page 1: Two modern-day firefighters of West Midlands Fire Service feel the heat during a realistic training session. (Edward Ockenden, West Midlands Fire Service)

Page 2: The dangers of firefighting are graphically illustrated in this dramatic view of a fireball exploding above a burning warehouse in Ipswich. (Sub Officer Harvey, Suffolk County Fire Service)

Right: A group of firemen struggling to get the available water onto one of the hundreds of outbreaks of fire experienced during the first few weeks of the London Blitz, September 1940. The tense expression on their faces tells it own story. (*Daily Mirror*)

Fire Services National Benevolent Fund
Marine Court
Fitzalan Road
Littlehampton
West Sussex BN17 5NF

Copyright © FSNBF 2003

This book was designed, produced and packaged by Stonecastle Graphics Ltd

Text by Neil Wallington
Design by Paul Turner and Sue Pressley
Edited by Philip de Ste. Croix
Printed by Tien Wah Press (Pte) Ltd

ISBN 0-95439-980-3

CONTENTS

FOREWORD

by Her Majesty Queen Elizabeth II

Patron – Fire Services National Benevolent Fund

BALMORAL CASTLE

The Chairman,
  The Fire Services National Benevolent Fund

The Fire Services National Benevolent Fund was born from modest beginnings during the drama and heroism of the London Blitz. Even in those early days, the Fund provided immediate care and help for the dependants of wartime firefighters who were killed or injured whilst saving life and property from the ravages of fire.

Since I became Patron in 1953 the Fund has continued to achieve great success, steadily developing its various facilities and available practical assistance, not only when a firefighter dies in action but also in support of families in times of serious illness and hardship.

The British Fire Service, and the selfless actions of its men and women firefighters at the scenes of countless fire and rescue emergencies over the years, are held in high regard by the public they serve.

In the Fund's Diamond Jubilee year, I send my warmest wishes to all those who are involved in this outstanding charity.

ELIZABETH R.

26th June, 2002.

1

PROLOGUE

Opposite: The fire service at work before the Second World War. Brass-helmeted firemen poised at the top of two 100-foot (30m) London Fire Brigade turntable ladders tackle a serious outbreak in a block of offices in Farringdon Street, EC4. Crews are also at work inside after having helped 30 workers to safety down ladders. Sadly, two office girls perished in the smoke. The date is 16 November, 1934.

THIS BOOK tells the remarkable human story of how, from very modest beginnings, The Fire Services National Benevolent Fund was set up to care for the families and dependants of firemen and firewomen killed and injured in the 1940 London Blitz, and in the subsequent bombing and fire raids of the Second World War.

Since that time, the Fund has grown to become a major charitable organization dedicated to serving the needs of modern-day firefighters and their families. *Out of the Flames* tells how the development of the Fund's services and facilities came about, and of some of the men, women and children whose lives have been helped by the Fund.

Inevitably, this story is inextricably linked to the dramatic work of the British Fire Service and stretches back over 60 years to those fiery, dramatic days of the savage air raids on the great cities and towns of the British Isles. Then firemen would stand in the streets with their water jets tackling that deadly enemy – uncontrolled fire rampaging loose as both incendiary and high explosive bombs relentlessly rained down.

Not that bombing was the only danger. If fire crews escaped the ear-shattering blasts of exploding bombs and red-hot shrapnel fragments whistling through the air, there remained a very high risk of being crushed under tons of debris as collapsing buildings, whose structures were weakened by fire and the concussion shock of the bombing, crashed to the ground. It was a hazardous business and one which soon led to the fire service being regarded as the "Fourth Arm" of the nation's armed forces. Early on during the 1940 London Blitz, Winston Churchill described firemen as "the heroes with grimy faces".

Today's firefighter has plenty of sophisticated high-tech equipment to rely upon, but this was not the case during the war years. At that time, there was little breathing apparatus, few radio sets – most messages and communications were delivered by fire service despatch riders – and firemen suffered dreadfully from a poor level of uniform personal protection. Throughout those dramatic wartime years, the risks were high. Apart from death and serious bodily injury, the intensity of physical and mental exhaustion that a firefighter had to withstand were of a nature which no modern firefighter can really comprehend.

From the start of the London Blitz in September 1940, the capital was raided continually by the *Luftwaffe* for 57 relentless days and nights. The badly bombed provincial centres were, where possible, reinforced by unaffected brigades from surrounding areas, but there were plenty of problems to add to the danger and fatigue of Blitz firefighting. For a start, the firefighting equipment of different brigades was not

*Early on during the 1940 London Blitz,
Winston Churchill described firemen as "the heroes
with grimy faces".*

In September 1940 during the first few days and nights of the London Blitz, the death and serious injury toll among London Fire Brigade personnel rose alarmingly.

The shape of things to come. A South London street scene in September 1940 during the first week of the Blitz.

always compatible. When pumps of the London Fire Brigade travelled in convoy to Coventry in November 1940, crews found that London hose would not couple up to Coventry's. Street water main standpipes were frequently of different size. Rank and command structures were unequal, and firefighting techniques and competence varied considerably from brigade to brigade.

Nevertheless, huge conflagrations had to be tackled and the demands upon fire crews to display courage, fortitude and self-sacrifice was of an order unlike anything previously experienced on the Home Front. In September 1940 during the first few days and nights of the London Blitz, the death and serious injury toll among London Fire Brigade personnel rose alarmingly. Right from the beginning, casualties afflicted both the professional crews of the London Fire Brigade, and the peacetime volunteers of its Auxiliary Fire Service (AFS) who had joined up at the outbreak of war in 1939 as part of the nation's reserve firefighting force. Overnight, entire families were left fatherless and without any means of ready support, either financial or emotional.

A few of the larger city brigades had some very modest pre-war welfare funds to provide basic aid in cases of suffering or hardship, but the vast majority of the 1,635 British fire brigades had no such provision. To deal with the numbers of London firemen being killed and injured in those first two weeks of the Blitz, a London Fire Service Benevolent Fund was quickly set up. Initially this was mostly funded by small donations from the public – at the end of the second week of September, the princely sum of £24 had been donated and sent to Brigade Headquarters at Lambeth.

As the ferocity of the German air raids intensified, the first donations started to arrive from American firemen whose Association had organized a coast-to-coast collection. Other monies began to arrive from the Commonwealth. Most of these donations were soon put to good use to support the families of the hundreds of London firemen and women who had become the victims of enemy action.

By the summer of 1941, it was obvious that the problem of operational incompatibility amongst the 1,635 UK fire brigades had to be urgently addressed. Senior fire service figures had been lobbying government ministers for some time and it was no surprise when nationalization of the British fire brigades brought about the establishment of The National Fire Service

(NFS) in August 1941. Soon after, a NFS Benevolent Trust was formed to coordinate the welfare needs of firefighters outside the London area.

Nationalization saw the beginnings of the modern-day service and ushered in standardization of equipment, national operational procedures, training, recruitment and rank structures. However, the NFS, which had a strength of 42,000 firemen and women by the end of the war, was never really tested by fire as the German bombing campaign weakened in the latter part of the war. Nevertheless, the intense flying bomb and V2 rocket attacks of 1944-45, mostly on London and the south-east, presented a new challenge to fire crews who

A ghostly view of a West Yorkshire firefighter amid the swirling smoke high above his colleagues as he tackles a major mill fire in the 1980s. (Brian Saville, West Yorkshire Fire Service)

Some of the dangers of firefighting are clearly illustrated in this 1958 picture of a serious fire in a department store in Manchester. Part of the frontage was weakened by the fire and it is suddenly crashing down into the street; fortunately, all the fire crews got clear in time.

were called upon to deal with the dreadful aftermath and carnage caused by Hitler's horror weapons.

This unification of UK fire brigades in 1941 also saw the first moves to centralize the administration of the now considerable benevolent and welfare needs of firemen and firewomen and their families. Thus it was that in August 1943, the National Fire Service Benevolent Fund was born, based around the considerable administrative experience gained over the previous two years by the London Fire Service Fund.

Nowadays, all 59 British fire brigades have a local Benevolent Fund network which ensures that an individual firefighter's needs are properly identified and met in a quiet and caring way.

Over 1,000 firefighters were killed during the Second World War and more than 7,000 seriously wounded.

Today, the Fire Services National Benevolent Fund (FSNBF) has grown from those modest beginnings to become an important part of the British Fire Service. Over the past 60 years the Fund has acquired and developed two convalescent homes, a rehabilitation and therapy centre, and various sheltered housing schemes. It supports more than 1,400 dependants, including widows and orphans, and provides practical help to the families of firefighters who are tragically killed or injured in the line of duty. Registered as a charity in 1948, a major landmark occurred in 1953 when HM The Queen graciously agreed to become the Fund's Patron.

Nowadays, all 59 British fire brigades have a local Benevolent Fund network which ensures that an individual firefighter's needs are properly identified and met in a quiet and caring way. For even in the modern age, firefighting and rescue still remains a dangerous business. Modern materials which emit toxic smoke when burning, and large and complex buildings present new dangers and challenges to today's fire crews. The fire service is also the nation's premier rescue service, usually first on the scene at serious road, rail and air crashes, chemical leakages and gas explosions. It is also called to rescue adults, children and animals trapped in various dangerous non-fire predicaments. The fire service also has to cope with responding to freak British weather conditions, such as flooding. Over the past 50 years, there has been an enormous growth in these non-fire emergencies and it is a fact that now the British Fire Service collectively rescues more men, women and children from such life-threatening incidents than from the old enemy – fire.

Apart from recognizing the foresight and energy of those who set up the FSNBF some 60 years ago, this book pays tribute to all those men and women who lost their lives in the fire defence of the country during the years of the Second World War, and to those who have since been killed and seriously injured serving the community in the front line of Britain's firefighting and rescue services.

Finally, in marking 60 years of the work of the FSNBF, *Out of the Flames* also acknowledges the courage, selflessness and commitment of all those who serve in the front line of the British Fire Service today and who stand ready to face danger, day and night, in all weather, on behalf of the community at large. Theirs, like their predecessors during the Blitz years, is truly a noble calling.

Neil Wallington
Bourne, Lincolnshire
September 2002

2 PRELUDE TO WAR

Many of the casualties died amid the smoke and flames of the conflagrations caused by the aerial attacks.

AS THE clouds of war gathered over Europe in the mid-1930s, it was clear to many senior officers in the large city fire brigades that aerial bombing of the civilian population of the United Kingdom by the German air force was very likely in the event of hostilities breaking out.

In 1937, during the Spanish Civil War, over 2,000 civilians were killed in the defenceless town of Guernica as a result of high explosive and incendiary bombing. Many of the casualties died amid the smoke and flames of the conflagrations caused by the aerial attacks.

In the same year as Guernica, the British parliament passed the Air Raid Precautions Act, which instituted a central fund to provide various civil defence measures, including a national reserve firefighting force entitled the Auxiliary Fire Service (AFS). The new Air Raid Precautions Act required the Home Office to meet most of the cost of these civil defence arrangements. Senior fire brigade officers estimated that to protect British cities from the likely effects of wartime air raids some 20,000 additional emergency pumps would be required to supplement those of existing fire brigades. Just as important would be the thousands of auxiliary firemen needed to man those additional pumps.

The AFS scheme envisaged that these reservist firefighters would be recruited and trained by regular fire offi-cers up and down the country. They would be ready to leave their normal occupations in the event of war to join the full-time fire brigades, rather like a Territorial Army of the fire service. Auxiliaries were enrolled in various cate-gories ranging from full firefighting duties to less-demanding work at ground level for the older recruits! There were special groups for those with experience to man fireboats on the Thames, and for women recruits who were expected to fill communication, administration and general driving duties.

Recruitment into the AFS began in London in March 1938 when plans were laid to enrol 28,000 auxiliaries to help man the fire defence of the capital. These would require 360 additional fire stations, most of which were to be requi-sitioned from existing buildings, such as schools, garages and small factories. But in the first months of 1938, AFS recruit-ment was slow. It took the Munich crisis later that year to prompt men to flock to fire stations to join the AFS.

In those pre-war years, the London Fire Brigade (LFB) was an all-profes-sional brigade of around 2,300 officers and men manning 55 fire stations and five river stations that provided fireboats on the River Thames. It was one of the largest, best-equipped and busiest opera-tional fire brigades in the world, and reg-ularly dealt with outbreaks of fire in huge river and dockside warehouses full

LONDON COUNTY COUNCIL
LONDON'S AUXILIARY FIRE SERVICE

INFORMATION
FOR INTENDING CANDIDATES

With war clearly on the horizon in the spring of 1939, hundreds of thousands of copies of this striking recruiting leaflet for the Auxiliary Fire Service were distributed across the London area.

15

16

August 1939. With the prospect of war close at hand, an AFS crew pose with their typical Austin taxi and Coventry Climax trailer pump outside the hastily requisitioned premises in Brompton, West London that housed their sub-station. They were lucky, as many other AFS crews found themselves based in pretty awful and unsanitary living conditions. (Author's collection)

of timber, rubber and other highly flammable materials. When regular London firefighters were joined by the first AFS basically trained volunteers in 1938, the combined force became known as the London Fire Service.

But the formation of the AFS continued to be dogged by difficulties, not just in London but across the country too. The Home Office was slow to issue uniforms, and suitable accommodation for AFS crews and their fire engines was slow in appearing – the process of requisitioning being particularly bureaucratic.

However, as the situation in Europe steadily deteriorated, the men and women recruits of the AFS started to see positive action in their preparation for war. The last "passing-out" parade of London AFS recruits after their 60 hours basic training occurred on 25 August, 1939. Five days later, steels helmets and respirators were issued to both LFB and AFS personnel. Sandbag filling began as blast protection measures were put in place at all 55 LFB regular fire stations and those AFS sub-stations which were in commission.

The Home Office finally announced the pay rates for AFS recruits who elected to join the full-time service on outbreak of war. These were £3 per week for men, £2 for women, 25 shillings (the equivalent of £1.25) for youths aged 17–18, and £1 for youths aged 16–17. The delay in confirming the pay scales must have had an impact on recruitment. It was one thing to ask men and women to commit themselves to a dangerous wartime duty involving leaving their peacetime jobs, but not being able to tell them the going rate of pay was another.

Nevertheless, in the last few days of peace a steady stream of AFS recruits registered at fire stations up and down the land to join up. Grey-painted Home Office AFS fire engines were now appearing on the streets. In London, 570 Home Office trailer pumps were delivered to LFB and AFS stations across the capital. And due to a shortage of suitable towing vehicles, over 2,000 Austin taxicabs were hired to pull these trailer pumps. This was an inspired move, for the London taxis were strongly constructed, had a small turning circle and

It was one thing to ask men and women to commit themselves to a dangerous wartime duty involving leaving their peacetime jobs, but not being able to tell them the going rate of pay was another.

were able to carry a four-man crew plus a good deal of hose and other equipment. In this way, many London taxi drivers along with their trusty vehicles also joined the ranks of the AFS .

On the communications front, the GPO (General Post Office) was urgently requested to install a network of telephone lines to connect all AFS sub-stations with their nearest LFB fire station – six AFS sub-stations in various requisitioned premises were attached to a parent regular fire station and its peacetime "patch".

When war was declared on 3 September, 1939, the AFS was mobilized and fire brigade readiness accelerated. In London, by noon on that fateful day, some 120 red LFB regular engines, 12 100-foot (30m) turntable ladders and a number of other specialist units, including five River Thames fireboats, stood ready. They were backed up by almost 2,000 AFS fire engines and trailer pumps based at over 300 sub-stations across the London area, manned by about 10,000 AFS personnel who were now part of the overall London Fire Service.

Some of the experiences of the first London AFS crews reveal the very real difficulty of finding suitable accommodation for the thousands of auxiliaries now called up. On 4 September, 1939 Fireman Vic Flint writing an entry in his diary from his AFS sub-station in an East London school recalled:

"No bombs and no fires! Which is pretty surprising to say the least. The first siren yesterday (a false alarm) put the fear of God into us. I must say I've never been so frightened in all my life. This is a miserable place and I've already caught two lice. One managed to get a couple of bites in before I killed it. This place is a London County Council Infant School, and I think the fire brigade must have brought the lice in along with the taxis, trailer pumps and telephones."

Others faced similar situations. AFS fireman "Mac" Young found himself posted to Winsland Street AFS sub-station in Paddington, West London. He was told that the sub-station was located in a requisitioned recreation hall belonging to the Great Western Railway. When he and his fellow crew members arrived at the hall, they found that GWR staff were still clearing it out; all the would-be firefighters had to camp in the nearby railway stables along with 200 restless horses and, as "Mac" recalled, about 10,000 GWR flies!

However, over the next few days and nights after the declaration of war, the AFS up and down the land began to deal with the hundreds of problems which confront any large volunteer organization that is suddenly faced with integration into its parent regular service. For

18

An AFS Fordson/Sulzer heavy pump pictured in Bethnal Green Road, London a few weeks before the outbreak of war in August 1939. These were capable of delivering 500 gallons (2,270 litres) of water per minute. Most AFS stations had at least one heavy unit and one trailer pump as their main firefighting weaponry. Finished in battleship grey, these government-provided fire engines lacked all the normal brass adornments of the regular pumps, but were to prove themselves powerful and reliable units. (London Fire Brigade)

many of the AFS personnel in smaller fire brigades, the difficulties of finding suitable requisitioned accommodation, the availability and issue of fire pumps, other vehicles and uniforms, continuation training, the preparation of operational communications, and many other problems tried patience and understanding on all sides.

But in the cities the pressures on the large professional fire brigades were even greater. They seemed unrelenting, particularly for the London Fire Service. Fortunately, after the first week of war had passed without incident, it became clear that there was not going to be a lightning strike by the *Luftwaffe*. The continuous duty system was replaced by watches. This protracted period of peace was really a godsend for all those involved in the organization of the AFS.

It allowed a much-needed consolidation period to build on the volunteers' earlier basic training and precious time to sort out the accommodation, equipment and uniforms still needed by London's reserve firefighting force. Recruitment into the AFS now grew to a positive flood. In the capital, 2,700 men and women joined the AFS during the first three weeks of September 1939.

The many logistical difficulties were as nothing compared to the problem of coordinating operational command and training of the auxiliaries. Surprisingly, at first the volunteers were not allowed to gain experience by attending the peace-time fires still being dealt with by the 2,500 professional firemen of the LFB. However, as 1939 gave way to the New Year, there were signs of real unrest in the AFS ranks. Personnel were subjected

Recruitment into the AFS now grew to a positive flood. In the capital, 2,700 men and women joined the AFS during the first three weeks of September 1939.

to endless training, exercises, and spit-and-polish sessions, and they had to endure cramped and, in many cases, totally unsuitable and unsanitary accommodation with the minimum of welfare facilities to ease the burden of the long hours of readiness. And still no war came to the Home Front.

Recognizing that this was an unsatisfactory state of affairs, the Chief Officer of the London Fire Service, Major Frank

Jackson, gave permission for some AFS crews to attend peacetime fires alongside regular LFB firemen to gain some real firefighting experience. Soon after midnight on the windy and bitterly cold night of 24 January, 1940, AFS pumps were mobilized as part of the first response to thick smoke pouring from a large warehouse in Oval Road, Camden Town. The fire on the first floor had taken a good hold and quickly developed

This 1935 Leyland was a typical example of a fire brigade pump in use by large professional city fire brigades at the outbreak of the Second World War. It carried a 50-foot (15m) escape ladder and 100 gallons (455 litres) of water. (London Fire Brigade)

During the pre-Blitz lull in June 1940, firewomen of the AFS undergo hose and hydrant drill during a training session at London Fire Brigade's Lambeth HQ. Primarily recruited for communications work and some driving duties, no woman formed part of a firefighting crew. However, many petrol-refuelling lorries and canteen vans were driven through the streets by firewomen throughout the raids. (London Fire Brigade)

into a 30-pump job, which brought a total of some 450 officers and firemen to the scene, including 300 AFS personnel, most of whom had not experienced such a serious fire at close quarters. The results were hardly surprising.

The fire was not under complete control until 1100hrs the following morning, by which time much of the huge structure of the warehouse had fallen in. Massive chunks of masonry and brickwork, together with huge sections of charred floor beams and joists, were scattered all around the site. In the mêlée of the night's battle, 12 firefighters were seriously injured, including five AFS personnel.

This single incident underlined the fact that the two firefighting forces in the capital, the regular LFB and the AFS, were still not properly integrated. There was clear antipathy between the two camps and this was not helped by the appointment of AFS officers from suitable members of their own ranks. Recruits who had joined the AFS from a professional background, such as the law or banking, soon found themselves with command and administrative responsibilities. With very little firefighting action after all the hectic build-up to war, it was hardly a surprise that in the spring of 1940 morale among AFS crews was plummeting to an all-time low.

It did not help that the popular press, notably the *Daily Mirror*, started to call the AFS a variety of names including "the Darts Brigade", "Duckers",

Massive chunks of masonry and brickwork, together with huge sections of charred floor beams and joists, were scattered all around the site. In the mêlée of the night's battle, 12 firefighters were seriously injured, including five AFS personnel.

"Parasites", "Idlers" and probably most cruelly "£3 per week Army Dodgers". The situation became so bad that many AFS firemen started to resign. Senior officers were unable to halt this stream, because the fire service was not, at that time, considered to be a reserved occupation. By the end of April 1940, many men had left the AFS to join the armed services to avoid the criticism being publicly aimed at AFS personnel.

But at that time Hitler's storm troops were already invading France and Belgium and the British Expeditionary Force was being remorselessly driven back to the Belgian coast. Ahead lay the Battle of Britain and the first campaign of aerial incendiary and high explosive bombing specifically targeted at the civilian population of London, the southeast and the provinces.

Within a very short period of time, the men and women of the fire service, both regulars and the AFS, would be hailed as national heroes everywhere they went, both on and off duty.

The fire service's first real brush with war. The London fireboat *Massey Shaw* and her crew sail up the Thames to a hero's welcome after making three round trips across the Channel to Dunkirk during which a total of 700 troops were rescued. The crew brandish their .303 rifles – their only armament! 4 June, 1940. (London Fire Brigade)

3

THE LONDON BLITZ BEGINS

BY THE end of April 1940, it was clear that war on the Home Front was not far away. Much of the British Expeditionary Force and units of the French and Belgian armies were progressively forced back and cornered along the coastline at Dunkirk by the rapid and unstoppable advance of German armour and infantry.

Months of anticlimax and inaction, together with public criticism of their value, meant that morale among AFS personnel in London and the south-east was at an all-time low. However, the evacuation of allied forces from the Dunkirk beaches brought about the first direct involvement of the fire service in the Second World War, and an end to the barren period of operational inactivity with which the many thousands of waiting AFS crews had had to contend.

The miles of dockland and river Thames frontage lined with huge warehouses and ships unloading cargoes of precious food and raw materials had long been identified as prime enemy targets. As a result, the London Fire Service had supplemented its three regular fireboats with a number of AFS-crewed vessels provided by the Home Office. They were based at strategic sites up and down the Thames. These boats were specialist craft with shallow draught, able to operate in tidal low-water conditions. Apart from their powerful deck-mounted water jets, the fireboats were also capable of pumping up to three tons of firefighting water per minute through hoses to supply fire engines ashore when normal supplies had failed.

On Thursday 30 May, the evacuation of the BEF was well under way. Many small boats were requisitioned and sailed across the channel to supplement the warships of the Royal Navy helping to evacuate troops from the Dunkirk beaches. This small armada of rescue boats were mostly petrol-driven. Alarmed at the fire risks that these vessels (now massing at Ramsgate) presented, the Admiralty requested the urgent use of an LFB fireboat to provide some sort of floating firefighting cover.

The fireboat *Massey Shaw*, based at Blackfriars Bridge, was immediately put on readiness. A volunteer crew was raised from firemen serving on the Thames. This consisted of an LFB station officer, two sub-officers and four firemen of the regular Thames fireboat service, together with six AFS firemen, a slightly larger crew than normal. *Massey Shaw* was the LFB's newest fireboat and was named after the brigade's famous Victorian Chief Officer. Commissioned in 1935, the vessel was 78ft (23.8m) long with a beam of 13ft (4m) and a shallow draught of only 3ft 9in (1.1m). Powered by twin 160hp diesels, *Massey Shaw* had a top speed in calm water of 12 knots.

When the fireboat arrived at Ramsgate at midday on 31 May, it became

The miles of dockland and river Thames frontage lined with huge warehouses and ships unloading cargoes of precious food and raw materials had long been identified as prime enemy targets.

Firemen struggling to get available water onto one of the hundreds of outbreaks of fire experienced during the first few weeks of the London Blitz, September 1940. The tense expression on their faces tells it own story. (*Daily Mirror*)

clear that all available vessels were being sent to the Dunkirk beaches. *Massey Shaw*, the only fireboat amid hundreds of other small craft, was directed to sail across the channel. With their .303 rifles and steel helmets as sole protection, the crew of the London fireboat set off on the crossing through the channel mine-fields, guided only by a hastily fitted, poorly calibrated compass and a growing pall of smoke that was towering over the Belgian and French coastlines ahead.

Arriving off Bray Dunes late on Friday afternoon, the crew quickly got a skiff to work ferrying soldiers from the queuing lines stretching out into the sea awaiting rescue. But the ebbing tide made the situation hazardous. After many attempts, a line was laid from a sunken lorry allowing a queue of Royal Engineers to climb aboard. So many clambered on deck that the *Massey Shaw* was in danger of capsizing, but eventually the fireboat was able to get under way, arriving safely back at Ramsgate early the next morning. 65 soldiers were disembarked, all were soaked through and most had been seasick.

Massey Shaw made two further trips to Dunkirk with the original crew relieved by fresh London firemen. The fireboat returned to Ramsgate on each

German bombers also started to hit the major oil refineries and fuel storage tanks along the Thames estuary at Thameshaven on the Essex shore.

occasion with a full load of exhausted soldiers. By the second and third trips, the organization on the beaches had improved, and for a while the fireboat ferried deckloads of troops to waiting Royal Navy destroyers operating from the mole.

When *Massey Shaw* finally came home upriver on Tuesday 4 June and sailed under Tower Bridge, the crew found a hero's welcome awaiting them. A nice touch was provided by LFB Chief Officer Major Frank Jackson who had arranged for the crew of the first Dunkirk trip to be taken out by launch. He also organized that many wives and family of the crews should be present at the mooring to greet their menfolk.

When the fireboat, with its full complement of Dunkirk veterans aboard, sailed upriver to moor at the fireboat pontoon at Brigade Headquarters at Lambeth, fire service history was made. Fortunately, no casualties had been sustained during the hectic days and nights of the operation, although the fireboat had suffered what the official report described as "various instances of collision damage".

After this initial excitement and taste of war in early June 1940, the London Fire Service braced itself for the air raids that were expected as a prelude to a German invasion attempt. It was not easy for the senior officers of the brigade to keep the AFS crews at the 360

sub-stations actively engaged while the red fire engines of the regular LFB dealt with the normal fire and emergency calls across the capital. Then the first enemy bombs fell in the fields of Kent, as the *Luftwaffe* began to test the air defences of the UK. They caused little damage. More bombs fell on open fields in Surrey and Hertfordshire in June and single air-raid warnings, broadcast to the London area by siren, became commonplace.

Once the Battle of Britain was joined in August 1940, sporadic heavy raids on RAF airfields took place. Croydon was one RAF station that was badly hit. Under the wartime regional

reinforcement scheme, the LFB sent ten pumps to help Croydon Fire Brigade deal with the huge fires in buildings around the perimeter of the airfield. German bombers also started to hit the major oil refineries and fuel storage tanks along the Thames estuary at Thameshaven on the Essex shore. 50 supporting pumps from London were dispatched to Essex to aid the hard-pressed local crews, and, this time, most of the London firefighters were drawn from the AFS, giving more than 200 firemen their first real baptism of fire.

AFS fireman James Gordon had been a journalist on the *Daily Telegraph* before the outbreak of war and he was one of those London firefighters on the convoy to Thameshaven. With the huge fires in the massive oil complex finally extinguished he recalled:

"The journey back to London the next day was a triumph. The road threaded through towns and suburbs where people turned and saw the grey and red appliances with their loads of oily men and hose. They cheered as they passed. Ginger stood up on the suction hose and took the cheers as though he was a prince and waved his arm in royal salute..."

London and Croydon Fire Brigade crews tackle a huge fire following a raid on Croydon RAF station during the Battle of Britain, August 1940.

Firemen were always in the front line during the raids. From the moment in September 1940 when London faced bombing for 57 consecutive nights of pyrotechnic hell, fire service casualties were high. This hose-laying lorry suffered a direct high explosive hit on 7 September, 1940 and was blown up into the roof of a row of terraced houses. No trace of the AFS crew was ever found. (*Daily Mirror*)

Unfortunately, the Thameshaven fuel installations were the target of the *Luftwaffe* on several further days. On the night of 24 August, 1940 during one of these raids to set fire to the Essex fuel tanks, two enemy planes apparently missed their target and instead dropped their mixed bomb loads of high explosive and incendiaries on parts of the City of London and the East End. The result was a fiery mayhem previously unseen in the capital.

One of the first high explosives struck the historic church of St Giles, Cripplegate. With scores of incendiaries clattering down into the roof ridges and gutters of nearby buildings in Fore Street, Barbican, many small yet intense fires were started high up in the fabric of the buildings. At first they were unseen from the streets below. The first crews on the scene, both regular LFB and AFS, soon had their hands full as uncontrolled fires spread in all directions. Down at the West India Docks where the second off-course bomber had dropped its load, firemen found a similar situation with fires blazing in two large dockside warehouses. Local fire stations were soon rapidly emptied of pumps, a fact that emphasized the potential fire threat to a wide area of London.

At Fore Street, 200 pumps were in use within the first hour. They were

It can only be imagined how the AFS crews, most of them being blooded for the first time, coped with the exposure to thick smoke, intense heat and flames, and the dangers of buildings suddenly collapsing…

mainly AFS heavy and trailer pumps, supported by a number of LFB red appliances. Many LFB firemen – despite their years of experience of inner-city firefighting – had never seen rapid fire spread. In peacetime, a 30-pump fire was reckoned to be a major incident. Down in the West India Docks, efforts were concentrated on trying to prevent two major fires from spreading. One required 100 pumps and two fireboats; the other nearby was attended by 70 pumps and six fireboats. Elsewhere in East London that night there was a 30-pump fire and a separate 20-pump incident. As if this was not enough, by 0100hrs on 25 August, the LFB had also been called to 48 minor fires, mostly on the roofs of unaffected premises, caused by the clouds of burning embers and sparks drifting from the conflagrations in the City and in the Docks.

It can only be imagined how the AFS crews, most of them being blooded for the first time, coped with the exposure to thick smoke, intense heat and flames, and the dangers of buildings suddenly collapsing after being weakened by severe fire. The sheer physical demands of such an intense firefighting effort over many hours called for Herculean endurance from all concerned.

Fortunately there was plenty of water as the mains were virtually unaffected by the bombing and the Thames was at high tide. Even so, the command

and control of the various incidents taxed the senior officers of the LFB to the limit. However, by mid-morning the following day, all the fires were under control. Nevertheless, many crews were required to stay at the scene to cool down debris and clear up several miles of intertwined hose, ladders and other equipment needed for the next raid.

The fire damage was widespread – entire streets were burnt out in the City and similar widespread devastation afflicted the Docks. But this momentous night had been the result of only two off-course aircraft. Just what would the massed squadrons of bombers be capable of during a sustained and prolonged aerial attack by hundreds of aircraft specifically targeting the capital city? The men and women of the London Fire Service were about to find out.

During the lull in 1940 before the Blitz, AFS crews were often derided by the press and public alike. But once the raids started, firemen found themselves dubbed by Churchill "heroes with grimy faces". Ben Betts, London AFS fireman, had been a Fleet Street cartoonist in peacetime, and in 1941 he published a book of cartoons of life in the London Fire Service. This is one of the most famous of them which found its way into newspapers around the free world.

4

A WELSH INFERNO

IT WAS not just the London Fire Service and fire crews in south-east England who first experienced enemy action when bombs strayed from their intended targets.

On 19 August, 1940 firefighters in West Wales had to contend with the aftermath of a single Junkers 88 bomber attack on the oil storage tanks at Llanreath, Pembroke Dock. Bombs struck a tank containing 12,000 gallons (55,000 litres) of oil. A huge fuel fire rapidly developed, spilling out as a running liquid fire which enveloped many adjacent larger tanks brimfull of flammable liquid. The mostly volunteer firemen of Pembroke Dock Fire Brigade soon had a massive conflagration on their hands. Despite reinforcements from fire brigades from other towns in West Wales, more tanks were soon burning out of control.

The fires rapidly threatened to ignite not only 17 storage tanks on the site, but also a number of nearby houses and other property as well. The situation was dire. During the first day, local crews and those from Milford Haven, Carmarthen, Haverfordwest and Swansea all pitched in with a concerted water and foam attack to try to isolate and extinguish the blazing tanks.

By early the next morning, the situation was so serious that fresh fire crews were ordered to Pembroke Dock by the Home Office from as far afield as Birmingham and the West Midlands. Cardiff Fire Brigade sent a convoy of ten pumps manned by 50 firemen who arrived at Pembroke Dock early on 21 August to support the weary local crews.

On the following day, with the oil tanks still burning out of control, the conflagration claimed its first victims. The thick steel of one of the burning cylindrical tanks, weakened and distorted by the high temperatures of the fire, suddenly buckled and collapsed, causing burning oil to gush out in a river of fire. Five Cardiff firemen were unable to get clear and were engulfed in flames. The fire was to burn on for almost three weeks before fire crews finally got the upper hand.

An aerial view of the huge fire involving the oil tanks at Pembroke Dock, West Wales, that broke out on 19 August, 1940 following a lone German raid. Here one of the burning tanks has "boiled over" sending a river of fire cascading in all directions. Five firemen were killed during this serious incident. (*Western Telegraph*)

Apart from the five fatalities among the Cardiff contingent, 38 other firemen were seriously injured during the three weeks of firefighting operations.

On 19 August, 2001 a memorial service was held at South Pembroke Golf Club on the site of the original oil tanks which were set ablaze by enemy air raid action on 19 August, 1940. It was three weeks before fire crews were able to bring the inferno under control. During this time five Cardiff firemen perished. Here, following the 2001 memorial service, representatives of serving and retired firefighters and their families stand behind the simple plaque which commemorates the tragedy.

By then, 22 fire brigades were in attendance, involving a total of about 650 firefighters. At Pembroke Dock they deployed 53 pumps and laid out nine miles of hose. Apart from the five fatalities among the Cardiff contingent, 38 other firemen were seriously injured during the three weeks of firefighting operations. In addition, some 1,153 separate medical treatments were needed, mostly for burns, cuts and grazes and the discomfort of hot oil entering boots. Of the 17 tanks at Llanreath, 11 were lost as were their contents of some 38,000,000 gallons (173 million litres) of precious oil.

Incredibly, this inferno, probably one of the largest fires in Great Britain for several centuries, was caused by a single bomber. The air defences of Pembroke Dock were virtually non-existent despite the fact that this was an oil tank site, and a major Coastal Command base for flying boats and deep-water harbour. Although the focus of the *Luftwaffe's* bombing might was about to be turned on London, this dramatic inferno in west Wales in August 1940 is remembered for the human sacrifice, suffering and sheer perseverance of the many fire crews who were involved in the three-week battle against the flames.

5 THE UNRELENTING RAIDS

At an early stage at West India Dock, thousands of gallons of rum spewed out of barrels across the surface of the docks and soon ignited, illuminating the scene and providing an awesome spectacle of the primeval power of fire.

FOLLOWING THE first "accidental" raid on central London on 24 August, 1940, the *Luftwaffe* continued to target the Essex oil installations at Thameshaven. A particularly concentrated raid took place on 5 September and, once again, the London Fire Service gave assistance dispatching a convoy of 50 pumps and their crews, mostly AFS personnel, to help the hard-pressed firefighters of the local brigades.

However, the entire German bombing strategy was about to change. As the nation rejoiced in the RAF's victory in the Battle of Britain, Hermann Goering directed that the principal target of the *Luftwaffe's* bombs would now be London. The German aircrews had a simple and chilling new operational directive – to raze Britain's capital city to the ground by fire and high explosive.

The first enemy raid on London came on Saturday 7 September, 1940 when the air-raid sirens wailed their preliminary warning at 4.33pm. Across London, fire crews stood ready rigged in their uniforms waiting for the detonations of falling bombs. Where would the enemy strike first?

Ten minutes later, there was no doubt as to the precise target area – the London Docks. Wave after wave of bombers swept up the line of the Thames from the east and high explosives and incendiaries rained down. Buildings within the Royal group of docks, Canning Town, Silvertown, East and West Ham and, on the south side of the Thames, Woolwich Arsenal with its large ammunition dumps were all "well alight" and threatening to spread.

Further up the river towards Tower Bridge, on the south side Surrey Commercial Docks took a heavy toll of bombs. Within five minutes of the first explosions, almost two million tons of imported softwood on the various quaysides was burning. Many hundreds of terraced houses and businesses in the streets next to these primary targets also suffered. Despite the rapid deployment of hundreds of firefighters around the dockland areas, the situation quickly grew worse. Such was the rapid and uncontrolled spread of fire inside the Royal Docks that within 30 minutes of the first bombs falling, West Ham Fire Brigade (just outside the London Fire Brigade area) was calling for 500 LFB pumps (about 2,500 firemen) in a first request for assistance. Unfortunately, by then London had problems of its own.

At the Surrey Docks, the initial attendance was 100 pumps, quickly augmented to 200 in an attempt to contain the spread of fire within a defined area. A particular hazard here were the flying burning brands from the stacked wood fires which took off downwind in the accelerating air current and drifted for several miles before dropping onto some unaffected roof, ledge or canopy to start

The scene on the morning after the intense raid on the City of London on 29 December, 1940. During that night 100,000 incendiaries were dropped on the City's square mile. Huge blazes were started and spreading fire progressively trapped about 80 firemen and their pumps in Whitecross Street, EC1 in the Barbican area. They were forced to abandon their pumps and flee the scene just before the entire street burned from end to end. (London Fire Brigade)

yet another fire. Major Jackson, Chief Officer of the London Fire Service, was forced to commit another 500 pumps into the worst fire zone. 250 were ordered to the north bank of the Thames below Tower Bridge, where lay London and St. Katharine's Docks, and the other 250 units were dispatched to West India Dock and its warehouses that were already burning from end to end. At an early stage at West India Dock, thousands of gallons of rum spewed out of barrels across the surface of the docks and soon ignited, illuminating the scene and providing an awesome spectacle of the primeval power of fire.

Peter Blackmore was a successful author and playwright who joined the AFS in 1939. On this first night of the London Blitz proper, 7 September, 1940, he was a crew member of one of the first reinforcing pumps into Surrey Docks. He later wrote:

"Eventually we came to a standstill at the wharf where we were to spend that endless night. Everything seemed to be on fire in every direction; even some barrage balloons in the sky were exploding. The cinder-laden smoke which drifted all around us made one think of the destruction of Pompeii."

Worryingly, this first targeted raid was just a brief one. The sirens sounded the merciful "all clear" at 6pm – the attack had only lasted for one-and-a-half hours. But the effect was devastating and it shocked even the professionals of the London Fire Brigade. Looking down the Thames from Charing Cross towards East London and its dockland, great spiralling clouds of acrid smoke intermittently obscured the fire glow from the infernos, and the reflected light lit up many miles of the London sky on either

In the streets, raging fires blocked off main roads. This obstacle combined with burning buildings crashing down onto the streets made it difficult for the reinforcing pumps to get close to where they had to be.

On the night of 29 December, 1940, the *Luftwaffe* dropped 100,000 incendiary bombs on the square mile of the City of London. At the height of the raid the Thames was at a very low ebb and water supplies were at a premium. A lone fireman waits for water at the top of a 100-foot (30m) turntable ladder.

side like some gigantic flickering electric storm; white ash fell from the skies.

Back at Regional Fire Control at Lambeth, the situation looked grim. By 6.30pm the scale of the firefighting task was becoming clear. Hundreds of pumps had already been deployed and the crew availability boards started to look decidedly empty as pumps from outlying brigades outside the London area were moved into the capital. The situation board showed no fewer that nine

conflagrations (a wartime fire service term meaning a fire officially out of control and spreading rapidly). In addition, the London Fire Service was simultaneously dealing with 19 other 30-pump, and 45 10-pump fires, plus over 1,000 smaller individual outbreaks of fire.

But on this first night of the Blitz, the *Luftwaffe* had not done with London yet. A fresh bombing alert sounded at 8.30pm and within minutes the bombs started falling again over an even wider

area. This time the City of London was badly hit and many commercial buildings close to the fire area of the 24 August raid were again set on fire. Fresh incendiaries fell on the docks and with London firefighters near to exhaustion, relief crews were ordered in from as far away as the Thames Valley and South Midlands regions.

In the streets, raging fires blocked off main roads. This obstacle combined with burning buildings crashing down onto the streets made it difficult for the reinforcing pumps to get close to where they had to be. Water supplies were at a premium, with many large-capacity mains pipes out of action through concussion damage. LFB and AFS fireboat crews performed sterling work in getting water ashore from the Thames across the low-tide mudflats. Broken gas mains burned everywhere. Even a rudimentary form of command and control was difficult to maintain. Many telephone lines to fire stations and street fire alarms were down, and virtually all messages and orders were carried by AFS motorcycle despatch riders. This was a relatively new wing of the London Fire Service and it certainly earned its spurs on this fiery and dramatic night.

More personal memories of firefighters on that first night of the London Blitz tell their own story. An AFS fireman at Rum Wharf, East India Dock recalled:

"The fires had a stunning effect. Wherever the eye could see, vast sheets of flame and a terrific roar. There was no need for headlights on the pump…The first line of big dockside warehouses was already alight from end to end…The fires were so huge that we could do little more than make an attempt to protect the adjoining buildings… The whole of the warehouse was a raging inferno against which we were silhouetted groups of pygmy firemen… Occasionally we would glance up at a strange sight, for a flock of pigeons kept circling round overhead almost all night long. It looked like sunrise all around us with the light from the huge fires, and the pigeons seemed white in the glare, birds of peace making a strange contrast with the scene below…"

Such was the widespread damage following the City raid of 29 December, 1940 that Winston Churchill ordered an immediate review of firewatching and air raid precautions in inner London. On the morning after the raid, Home Secretary Herbert Morrison MP takes an aerial look at the fire-damaged area from the top of an LFB 100-foot (30m) turntable ladder close to the Bank of England. Below him are many pumps still at work damping down. The hoses of water relays stretch in all directions into the distance – testament to many battles won and lost the previous night. (*Daily Mirror*)

In the streets, seven London firemen had been killed and over 200 had been seriously injured. It was a taste of what was to come during the next 57 nights of ordeal by fire…

A regular LFB officer was bringing a small convoy of fireboats back up the river after several days of firefighting at the most recent Thameshaven oil tank raid. As the fireboats came into Woolwich Reach, the raid was well under way. Before them stood an extraordinary spectacle. He recalled:

> "There was nothing but fire ahead, apparently stretching right across the Thames in front of us and burning on both its banks. We seemed to be entering a tunnel of fire with no break in it anywhere. All the usual landmarks were obliterated by walls of flame. Burning barges drifted past us…
>
> At one stage, we were getting into position to fight a fire in a large warehouse when the entire riverside front of the building suddenly crashed into the river towards the fireboat with an almighty splash. The warehouse contents appeared to be sacks of beans, and for some minutes they cascaded into the water making a loud noise like a tropical rainstorm…"

Through all this pyrotechnic hell, firefighters stood their ground in the streets even as the bombs continued to fall. They struggled for hours on end to get the available water to their pumps and then onto the flames, putting up huge water curtains to try to restrict fire spread to unaffected buildings. Many crews could not be relieved to take proper refreshment until dawn had broken and the raid appeared to be over. Eventually, a number of canteen vans, manned by firewomen, were able to venture out into the streets and set up on street corners, each a little oasis of hot drinks, soup and sandwiches for the exhausted firefighters. Most were dehydrated and many suffered from the effects of a form of conjunctivitis caused by prolonged exposure to swirling smoke, embers, ashes and dust suspended in the atmosphere. During the morning, hospitals set up special treatment areas where the injuries were treated.

There was also a pressing need to refuel the pumps which had been running flat out for many hours. Hose reserves were already stretched to the limit. Most firefighters were soaked to the skin and few of the AFS crews had a second dry uniform back at the fire station to change into. However, by 5am in the morning, the final "all clear" of the night sounded and some semblance of control was gained over the hundreds of fires. A brief entry in the London Fire Service war diary that morning was a masterpiece of understatement. Bearing in mind that London Fire Control had logged over 1,000 separate serious fires that night, the diary simply read:

The classic painting of Blitz firefighting action entitled "Wall Falling on Two Firemen, 1940". It was painted by Leonard Rosoman RA during his service as a wartime London AFS fireman, and captures the danger of firefighting under extreme wartime conditions. (Imperial War Museum)

"Night of September 7/8, 1940: A big and prolonged raid caused great fires at Surrey Docks, East and West India Docks, the Royal Arsenal at Woolwich, the City of London and elsewhere which taxed the whole of the London Fire Service."

At that stage, the cost in human lives of this first Blitz raid was not readily known. Some hours later, it became clear that 430 men, women and children had been killed in their homes, mostly from bomb blast and perishing under collapsed structures.

In the streets, seven London firemen had been killed and over 200 had been seriously injured. It was a taste of what was to come during the next 57 nights of ordeal by fire, both for the population of London and for the men and women of its already battered fire service.

6 GENESIS

Opposite: Another vehicle casualty of the London Blitz, 10 May, 1941. This Commer towing unit and trailer pump has come to grief in a bomb crater amid smoke and sparks on the south side of Southwark Bridge. The crew escaped with minor injuries. Note the hose relays (left) taking much-needed water to the north side of the river to cope with hundreds of fires in the City district. (London Fire Brigade)

DURING THE first dark days and nights of the London Blitz in September 1940, the numbers of regular and AFS London firemen killed and injured during bombing raids grew alarmingly. By the end of the first two weeks of bombing, 52 firemen had fallen in action. 501 had been seriously injured. The majority of the fire service casualties were married men who left widows and children. Apart from the enormous mental trauma caused by such loss, the dependants faced other immediate difficulties, financial and otherwise.

For the widows of regular firemen killed in action, state aid was minimal. Quite incredibly, at the beginning of the London Blitz there was no specific fire service death grant provision for any widow whose AFS husband had been killed in wartime firefighting operations. At first, no members of the AFS were provided with state assistance if they were seriously injured. Even regular firemen were subject to means-testing to obtain benefits for their dependants, and they received no special treatment despite being in the front line of the nation's home defences.

By the middle of September 1940, as the intense day and night air raids continued on an unrelenting daily basis, the fire service casualties grew. It was not surprising that the growing numbers of fire service family hardship cases had become a serious cause for concern for

*Quite incredibly, at the beginning of the London Blitz
there was no specific fire service death grant provision for
any widow whose AFS husband had been killed in
wartime firefighting operations.*

By 8 October, 1940, the death toll of London firefighters had grown to 70 firemen and three firewomen, with over 750 seriously injured through enemy action.

Above and opposite: In the execution of their duty, several hundred firemen lost their lives in the 1940-41 London Blitz. Here the camera records two separate simple and moving lying-in-state ceremonies as colleagues pay their last respects and mourn their sacrifice.

40

London's fire chief, Major Frank Jackson, and his officers.

Although burdened by the heavy responsibility of ensuring that London's fire defences held firm against what must have seemed overwhelming odds, Jackson personally took the question of the meagre financial provisions made for firefighters killed and injured in action directly to the Home Office, the Whitehall department with responsibility for the fire service. The Home Secretary, Herbert Morrison, was sympathetic, and undertook to take the matter up with the Ministry of Pensions.

By then, the Fire Brigades Union was also bringing great pressure to bear upon both the government and fire authorities up and down the country to improve the provisions for firefighters killed and injured in action.

As a result of this lobbying, some improvements came about fairly quickly. In London, an existing pre-war funeral allowance of £7.10s.0d (the equivalent of £7.50) granted to the widows of regular fireman killed on duty was extended to cover all firefighters. Injury pay started to be paid for a period of up to eight weeks, and this was extended to 13 weeks if no physical recovery was deemed likely. Better still, the odious system of means-testing firefighters and their families prior to the award of injury pay was abolished. However, during the first few weeks of the London Blitz there were still many instances of firefighters, their widows and families suffering extreme hardship and distress.

The unrelenting daily air raids taxed the entire resources of the London Fire Service. By 8 October, 1940, the death toll of London firefighters had grown to 70 firemen and three firewomen, with over 750 seriously injured through enemy action. Clearly some support scheme other than the complicated government aid package was desperately needed. It needed to be able to respond quickly with financial and welfare support for those members of the fire service and their families most in need.

At about this time small cash donations started to be handed in by members of the public at various London fire stations. These modest funds were passed to Headquarters on the Albert Embankment opposite the Houses of Parliament. By the second week of September 1940, a total of £24 had been received in donations and collections. Alongside all his strategic firefighting responsibility, Major Jackson had to consider how best to set up a mechanism to distribute the sums that were starting to flow in. He decided that a Benevolent Fund of some sort should be established for the men and women of the London Fire Service, and he asked a small representative group of LFS personnel to examine how this proposal could best be achieved.

...the odious system of means-testing firefighters and their families prior to the award of injury pay was abolished.

"Incendiaries" by Paul Dessau. A fine painting by an artist who joined the AFS in 1939 and whose work was included in the various exhibitions of firemen's artwork staged in London on behalf of the London Benevolent Fund, and later for the NFS Fund.

41

Only two days later, District Officer Ronnie Greene was one of a small team who attended that inaugural committee meeting and so set in train a series of events which led to the birth of the Fire Services National Benevolent Fund.

7 A FUND FOR LONDON

THE INAUGURAL management committee of the London Fire Service Benevolent Fund met at Lambeth Headquarters on 2 October, 1940. The meeting convened under the chairmanship of Commander Ken Hoare, one of the LFB's senior officers and a very experienced firefighter with a deserved reputation of leading from the front. Apart from Ronnie Greene, who agreed to become the new Fund's Honorary Organizing Secretary, the two other members of the group were Charles Giveen and Betty (later Lady) Cuthbert, a senior woman officer, who represented the interests of the fire-women of London's Fire Service.

Before the war, the London Fire Brigade had a long established Amateur Athletic Association (AAA) which had regularly organized a number of track and field events at the White City stadium in West London. These meetings were staged not only for the brigade's own athletes, but also for participants from athletic clubs across the capital. To help fund this activity, regular LFB members of the London Fire Service had long been contributing sixpence (the equivalent of 2.5p) a week towards the brigade's AAA and its various events. When it became clear that athletic activities would have to cease during the war years, the regular sixpenny weekly donations ceased.

At the beginning of the inaugural meeting, Ken Hoare announced that it had been unanimously agreed that the London Fire Service AAA sixpenny weekly subscription was to be restarted with the proceeds going directly towards the new Fund.

By the end of September, personnel serving at eight of London's fire stations had contributed a total of £15.16s.0d. (£15.80) to augment the £24 of public donations already received. Donations from this internal source quickly accelerated and by the time the new management committee met again on 9 October, 1940, some £130 had arrived by this route to add to the growing total of public donations.

The records show that from its inaugural meeting up to the end of that year, the London Fire Service Benevolent Fund (LFSBF) provided direct and rapid assistance for 298 individual "cases" with grants totalling £977.16s.0d (£977.80). A salutary note records that by the end of October 1940, £88.4s.0d (£88.20) had been spent on funeral wreaths. This gives some idea of fire service casualties during the early weeks of the London Blitz.

Income reaching the London Fund via donations and collections to the end of December 1940 totalled £3,354. This included £403 from the resumed sixpenny LFSAAA donations, £483 directly from the funds of the LFSAAA, and £1,555 from public donations handed in

The records show that from its inaugural meeting up to the end of that year, the London Fire Service Benevolent Fund (LFSBF) provided direct and rapid assistance for 298 individual "cases".

"Rescue of Horses" by Reginald Mills. An evocative work by this London AFS fireman artist. During the war many companies in London used horse transport, and horses frequently had to be rescued from burning stables during Blitz raids. Reginald Mills also painted the watercolour reproduced on the cover of this book, which was used as the basis of the FSNBF logo in 1948.

43

at fire stations or sent by post to Lambeth HQ. Some idea of Fund Secretary Ronnie Greene's energy can be gained from the proceeds of a Christmas 1940 Draw which he personally found time to organize. It produced a handsome profit for the Fund of £912.

Ronnie Greene's own notes from that time throw an interesting light on the London Fund's early growth during a time when the bombs were still falling:

"The Fund operated in those days on the basis of small local

44

Above: In September 1940 the London Fire Service Benevolent Fund was set up to distribute the first public donations to the widows and families of firemen killed and seriously injured in the Blitz. By 1941 the Fund was receiving a steady flow of money and some very large donations started to arrive from the United States and Commonwealth countries. This certificate, dated 9 April, 1941, was presented by an American Firefighters Association to a Fire Department in Lebanon, New Hampshire, and recognizes the donation made to the British Fire Fighters Relief Fund. At that time this Fund was being primarily administered alongside the London Benevolent Fund, prior to the development of the national scheme. (Bob Fitz, retired Chief, Lebanon Fire Department, New Hampshire, USA)

Right: During the London Blitz raids, high explosive bombs did enormous damage to firefighting water mains and other utility services. This view, looking north up Tottenham Court Road, W1 on 24 September, 1940, was taken during the third week of continual raiding. (London Fire Brigade)

The Minute Book for 3 January, 1941, for example, tells us that 26 auxiliary firemen and women were helped and that death grants were paid to the widows of four firemen killed the day before.

46

Opposite: A building with all six floors well alight during the intense night raid which marked the end of the first phase of the London Blitz. This is the Elephant and Castle, SE1 on 10 May, 1941. (London Fire Brigade)

committees, prompt action, sympathetic treatment and helpful advice, and all grants being paid **immediately** in cash. In those days there was always a sense of great urgency; night after night there were heavy raids, and day after day new tragedy and hardship followed in their wake."

The Minute Book for 3 January, 1941, for example, tells us that 26 auxiliary firemen and women were helped and that death grants were paid to the widows of four firemen killed the day before. Of course, excellent liaison was quickly established with the WVS and Red Cross; their help in kind was invaluable to fire service families.

Thus the work continued into 1941. As the income of the London Fund steadily grew, so help could be increased. As a result of the Fund's progressively swelling income, a four shillings (20p) per week per child orphans' allowance scheme was introduced to supplement the basic financial death grants paid to London Fire Service widows.

What the members of the inaugural committee together with Ronnie Greene and his small administrative team had achieved in such a short space of time was quite remarkable. However, greater nationwide challenges and tasks lay ahead in providing for the dependants of Churchill's "heroes with grimy faces".

*What the members of the inaugural committee
together with Ronnie Greene and his small administrative
team had achieved in such a short space of time was
quite remarkable.*

8

RONNIE GREENE – HIS WORK AND TIMES

RONNIE GREENE was born on 25 September, 1899 at the Woodman Public House on London's Highgate Hill. Times were often hard in the family as he was growing up. As a young boy, Ronnie took various odd jobs to help out with the family budget, including walking the dog of the Sainsbury's grocer family.

In 1916 Ronnie joined the regular army and after training he was posted to the London Scottish Regiment, later transferring to the Coldstream Guards where, no doubt, the considerable spit-and-polish and drill discipline of the foot guards was to stand him in good stead in years to come.

Ronnie left the army in 1919 and trained for a while as a biochemist. When his father died, he looked for work in the evening to supplement his daytime job. After starting work at a nightclub in London's West End, Ronnie seemed to get a taste for the nightlife and within a few years he gave up being a chemist. By then he had been appointed manager of the famous Café de Paris where he organized some of the most successful society tea dances of the 1920s and other entertainment.

Besides his nightclub work, Ronnie continued to look for other ways of augmenting the family income. In 1928, an opportunity came to take up exhibition free-fall parachute jumping. He recalled that he was always scared stiff as the pilot of the aircraft frequently seemed to be the worse the wear for drink. Bearing in mind how primitive parachute equipment was in those days, it is clear that Ronnie was not one to duck a tough physical challenge.

However, Ronnie's daring and dangerous involvement with parachute jumping came to an end when the craze for the Black Bottom and Charleston dances started to sweep the nation. At the Café de Paris, Ronnie joined his good friend, the bandleader Victor Sylvester, to stage exhibition dancing. This enterprise soon led to Ronnie entering competitive dancing championships himself. He eventually became World Charleston Champion, a title he held until the craze died out a few years later.

By then Ronnie had also become involved commercially in the boot and shoe trade, before deciding that his business acumen could be better used elsewhere. This led him to get involved in the world of speedway racing which, in 1930, was attracting huge crowds to tracks up and down the country. Immediately he rode on the cinder track at Bristol, Ronnie was hooked by the whole noisy, exciting atmosphere of speedway racing. But he could also see the considerable commercial potential for the sport. By early 1936, Ronnie had become the promoter of Bristol Speedway. In 1937 he moved to become the commercial promoter of the

*Immediately he rode on the cinder track at Bristol,
Ronnie was hooked by the whole noisy, exciting
atmosphere of speedway racing.*

Wimbledon Speedway, one of London's premier tracks.

Thus began Ronnie's long and successful reign at Wimbledon which was only interrupted by the gathering clouds of war over Europe. By 1938, along with many other Londoners, Ronnie had enrolled as a fireman in the Auxiliary Fire Service.

By the time that Ronnie had completed his basic 60-hour training and had been posted to a fire station, events on the international stage were moving fast. When war was declared on 3 September, 1939, full mobilization of the AFS up and down the land was set in motion. In the London area, there was an urgent need for the 20,000 AFS firemen and women to complete their training and be properly billeted, fed, supplied and generally forged into a truly effective firefighting force.

There were simply not enough professional officers in the regular London Fire Brigade to undertake this task, and the Home Office agreed that certain AFS recruits who had a suitable background and experience in the general management of businesses could be promoted as rank holders and given responsibility for a particular section of AFS development and training.

Ronnie Greene, with his successful experience of running Wimbledon Speedway, found himself among this group. By 1940 he held the rank of

WIMBLEDON SPEEDWAY
PHOTO-ALFA STUDIOS

The father of the Fund, Ronnie Greene, pictured in 1938 when he was the promoter of Wimbledon Speedway. (*Vintage Speedway* magazine)

49

Column Officer. One particular requirement of the AFS recruitment and development campaign was the enrolment of qualified motorcyclists to form a small group of mobile messengers. It was quickly realized that in the event of war the AFS and the professional London Fire Brigade would not be able to rely upon the basic GPO telephone system and the street-corner fire alarms posts as the main means of communication. These vital links would be vulnerable to bombing raids.

Ronnie used his extensive links within the London motorcycle fraternity, and

One particular requirement of the AFS recruitment and development campaign was the enrolment of qualified motorcyclists to form a small group of mobile messengers.

Above: Ronnie Greene poses with his 1939 Wimbledon Speedway team. (*Vintage Speedway* magazine)

Right: District Officer Ronnie Greene MBE. This photograph was taken in January 1941 to mark the award recognizing his work in setting up the London Fire Service Benevolent Fund. The picture was taken in the first offices of the London Fund at 94 Southwark Bridge Road, SE1.

Ronnie's tireless work in setting up the London Benevolent Fund was honoured by the King in the 1941 New Year's Honours List with the award of an MBE.

On 16 October, 1940, while the London Fire Service was still taking a nightly battering from the *Luftwaffe*, HM The King paid a visit to Lambeth HQ to talk to various crews and see for himself how the LFS was coping. Here the King inspects a group of AFS despatch riders. This important and very successful communications division was set up in 1940 by District Officer Ronnie Greene (on the King's left) drawing on his pre-war contacts and experience as the promoter of Wimbledon Speedway. (London Fire Brigade)

soon formed a corps of despatch riders from the ranks of the AFS. They became Fire Service Despatch Riders (DRs), ready to carry vital operational information through the streets when all normal communications had failed. At first the DRs used their own motorcycles, until sufficient requisitioned and new machines became available. By the summer of 1940, each LFB division had up to a dozen AFS DRs attached. Their initial basic training was carried out at New Cross Speedway stadium! Ronnie also created a small group of firewomen DRs from the ranks of women drivers, something that even the armed forces had not done by that stage of the war.

When the raids of August and September 1940 began, Ronnie was attached to Divisional Commander's Staff HQ at Shoreditch and was involved in the supervision of Blitz firefighting and general deployment of fire crews, together with the development of the DR corps.

Ronnie's tireless work in setting up the London Benevolent Fund was honoured by the King in the 1941 New Year's Honours List with the award of an MBE. From then on, the provision of proper care and welfare facilities for his fellow firefighters was to be the main focus of the rest of Ronnie Greene's life. His time was to be devoted to the care and welfare of fellow firefighters and their dependants across the nation.

9

THE NATIONAL FIRE SERVICE

A firestorm developed around the city centre when vast amounts of air were sucked in to feed the flames of the many fiercely burning buildings.

WHEN 57 nights of continual bombing came to an end in November 1940, the London Fire Service was physically exhausted by the efforts of endless firefighting operations and damping-down duties at the scenes of thousands of fires across the Greater London area. But the thin red line held.

Sporadic raids continued through December 1940 and into the early months of 1941. Although *Luftwaffe* aircraft still droned across London skies loaded with a deadly cargo of high explosive and incendiaries, the bombing took on a more irregular pattern. This at least gave fire crews some relief and rest from the physical and mental demands of the almost non-stop raids of the autumn of 1940.

However, London was not the only strategic centre to be bombed during the early months of the Blitz. On 14 November, the city of Coventry suffered a particularly heavy raid which lasted 11 hours. Coventry Fire Brigade worked tirelessly to try to contain the fires for some four hours but they were slowly overwhelmed by the deteriorating situation. Matters soon became critical.

A firestorm developed around the city centre when vast amounts of air were sucked in to feed the flames of the many fiercely burning buildings. Downwind, huge sparks were carried up on the convection currents, only to drift down some distance away onto buildings as yet unharmed, so starting even more rooftop fires. Much of the city centre including its historic cathedral burned from end to end. With all local telephones out of action, requests for assistance took precious time to action.

Although pumps came to Coventry as quickly as they could from the surrounding fire brigades of the West Midlands, confusion reigned. Faced with an ever-worsening fire situation, no proper command and control coordination could be established, the deployment of fresh crews was haphazard, and firefighting water resources were minimal. Worse still, some of the hose connections of the relief brigades arriving at the Coventry conflagration were incompatible with those of neighbouring forces. In 1939 London and several of the large city brigades had been reluctant to adopt hoses with a new type of "snap together" coupling, preferring to rely upon the well proven screwed coupling hose which had been in use since the early part of the century.

When news reached the Home Office of the dreadful situation in Coventry, 50 London firemen were sent there in London buses. They arrived in the early hours of 15 November, but could not find any fire pumps or hose to use. It had been a folly to send them without their pumps. In any case, by then much of Coventry's city centre, including its cathedral, was burnt out.

Although larger convoys of pumps were eventually dispatched to Coventry from as far away as London and Manchester, they were too late to be of much use. Trevor Hughes was a London auxiliary who travelled with the London convoy. This consisted of pumps, hose-laying lorries, utility lorries and despatch riders. He recalled:

"Nearing the city centre, we came upon some tired looking Coventry firemen at a canteen van. 'How did you get on?' we asked. One fireman shrugged his shoulders. 'Most of them got it in the head or chest with the shrapnel. There were 13 killed just working round one pump…

We finally came upon the centre, past a tramcar battered, burnt out and abandoned. Here the streets had apparently disintegrated into mighty and unending mounds of broken brick and glass, and writhing, black smouldering shapes of ironwork and wood…

Then we met more local firefighters. They drifted past our pumps, not recognizing friends, not talking amongst themselves, walking slowly,

October 1941. Only two months after the formation of the National Fire Service, representatives of the South African government presented a mobile canteen unit to No 5 Region (London). After the ceremony a short display was staged including pump and ladder drills and an exhibition by 16 NFS motorcycle despatch riders. Eight of these were firewomen – the left hand line in the photograph.

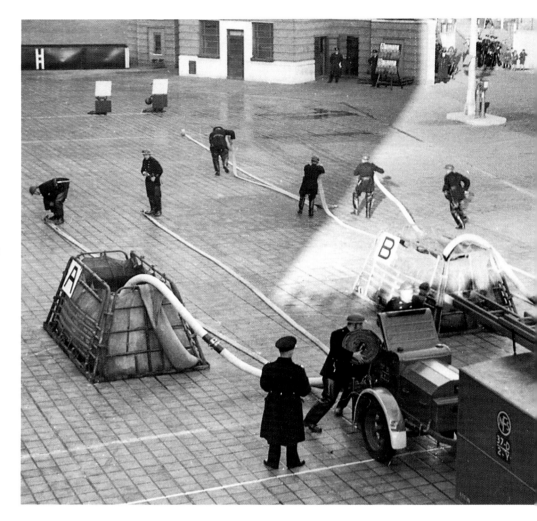

The display also included a trailer pump competition with teams of firemen from across the region competing against the clock to get two lines of hose to work.

silently with mechanical steps and unseeing eyes; lost ghosts moving along the well remembered shadows of a fallen city. Their eyes were tired and bewildered, their minds numbed by pain, shock and horror unimaginable. But none gave any signs of despair."

The Coventry raid taught one vital lesson – if firefighting assistance was to be sent to a distant region, it had to be assembled and got moving quickly if it was to be of any use. A week after the Coventry raid, Birmingham was bombed quite badly; a London convoy of 15 pumps was on its way north within an hour of the request for help.

During this time, the *Luftwaffe* switched its attacks between London and the main ports. Southampton was the target of several big raids during the last week of September, and with its firemen under pressure, convoy reinforcements were dispatched from the larger Home Counties brigades and from London. Commander Firebrace, the Chief Regional Fire Officer based at the Home Office, also sent a London regular officer, Divisional Officer Arthur Sullivan, on an urgent mission to Southampton to see how the fire pump convoys and the overall command of such large Blitz fire areas could be made more effective.

Sullivan's report highlighted more

A central firefighting organization with a considered strategy was clearly needed but there was initial resistance to such an idea in Whitehall.

approach to the Home Secretary. Jackson decided that the most effective way forward would be for a small group of his London officers with convoy experience to tell their stories directly to government officials. The officers included John Fordham, Geoffrey Blackstone and Ken Hoare (the first Chairman of the London Fire Service Benevolent Fund who was later to become post-war Chairman of the Fund when it became a national organization).

Several days elapsed before this small group was able to meet Sir George Gater, the secretary to the Ministry of Home Security. Also present at the meeting were Sir Arthur Dixon, head of the fire service division at the Home Office, and Commander Aylmer Firebrace, the pre-war chief officer of the London Fire Brigade, now Chief of the Fire Staff and Inspector in Chief. The London officers, all very experienced in convoy operations, were asked what they felt was the best strategy for the fire service under war conditions. There was one unanimous reply – nationalization.

While this lobbying was going on, raids on both London and the hard-pressed provinces continued and the groundswell of opinion for improvement within the fire service grew. Letters began to appear in *The Times* and the *Daily Telegraph* pointing out the inadequate firefighting provision in some parts of the United Kingdom. Questions

examples of the firefighting difficulties encountered during the Coventry Blitz. It drew attention to the staggeringly varying standards and designs of firefighting equipment, the disparate command and control systems, the widely varying rank structures and training competencies of fire brigades up and down the country. All this needed sorting out as a matter of great urgency.

A central firefighting organization with a considered strategy was clearly needed but there was initial resistance to such an idea in Whitehall. During March 1941 while moderate raids on London and the provinces were still taking place, several senior LFB officers lobbied their Chief, Major Jackson, to make an urgent

On 19 April, 1941, not long before the NFS Bill was introduced into the Commons, 34 firemen and firewomen were killed when a school in Poplar, east London, received a direct hit by a high explosive bomb.

were asked of the Home Secretary in the House of Commons when he admitted that the constant pressures on firemen were similar to those experienced in a "military operation".

Matters came to a head on 18 April, 1941 when, in the early evening, Herbert Morrison summoned Sir George Gater, Sir Arthur Dixon and Commander Firebrace to a conference at the Home Office. The meeting lasted until the early hours. From this gathering the National Fire Service (NFS) was born. Hurried consultations then followed with local authorities about plans for a unified fire service. On 13 May, only three days after London had suffered the most prolonged and intense Blitz raid of the entire war, the Fire Service (Emergency Provisions) Bill 1941 was introduced in the Commons.

Introducing the Bill, Home Secretary Herbert Morrison told a hushed and attentive Commons:

"Firefighting in the provinces is on a totally different basis from London where the county council maintain a vast firefighting machine, very similar to the army or navy. At the other end of the scale, in one provincial county borough there is only an establishment of 32 firemen. In another town, heavily attacked by the enemy, there are no fewer than 12 volunteer firemen.

The real weakness of the country's fire defence is the small units."

While all this backroom work was going on in Whitehall and elsewhere to create a national firefighting force, the dangers of wartime firefighting were once again underlined by two particular incidents in London.

On 19 April, 1941, not long before the NFS Bill was introduced into the Commons, 34 firemen and firewomen were killed when a school in Poplar, east London, received a direct hit by a high explosive bomb. Twenty one of the dead were AFS firemen from Beckenham in

Kent who had not long arrived at the school on relief duties. This awful tragedy still stands today as the largest single loss of uniformed firefighters in Great Britain.

The Poplar incident occurred only three weeks before another Blitz tragedy. On 10 May, 1941, 17 London firemen had died at the site of the Surrey Music Hall near the Elephant and Castle in south London. This was the night of a huge raid which signalled the end of the intense London Blitz.

By the time of the Fire Service Bill's second reading on 11 June, 1941, Morrison confirmed that the operational strength of the AFS was 80,000 full

timers and 150,000 personnel giving part-time cover.

It took only a week for the Bill to go through its committee stages and to receive Royal Assent. This cleared the way for the amalgamation of all United Kingdom fire brigades into a structure divided into 12 regions, each being sub-divided into fire force areas. The government continued to meet the entire cost of the AFS element of the new NFS, and to fund one quarter of the normal cost of the former professional brigades. Herbert Morrison also gave an undertaking to return fire brigades to local authority control at the end of hostilities.

A contingent of firemen of the National Fire Service briskly enters the Mall during a United Nations march through central London on 14 June, 1942. This representative group of firefighters was drawn from fire forces across the UK.

60

The NFS formally came into being on 18 August, 1941. Herbert Morrison issued the first order of the day to the men and women of the new force:

"On the day the NFS comes into being and you take your place in the ranks of the nation's unified fire service…
You stand in the front rank of our defence against the menace of air attack. You have already faced tasks such as no fire brigades in the world's history have ever been called upon to perform…
Now you step forward into a new service planned to meet the grave tasks which lie ahead. The present change is being made in order to weld the many fire services into a single national service, which can be more effectively organized, trained and directed for large-scale firefighting operations…
In the name of the nation whom you have served and will serve so well, I thank you for what you have done, and I charge you: Train, Organize, Practise and Be Ready."

History recalls that, paradoxically, the new NFS was never really tested by fire, for the huge London raid of 10 and 11 May, 1941 marked the end of the very intense German air attacks on Britain. The sporadic bombing of London and

the provinces in 1942 and 1943 still provided challenges for the NFS, and by then the new firefighting organization was benefiting from a much-needed consolidation in all areas of its work.

Tragically the NFS was only a few days old when its first fatality occurred. NFS units had been called to a ship fire at South Shields. Divisional Officer George McGregor, the Fire Force Commander of the Newcastle area, was in charge of firefighting and as he was leading a breathing apparatus team down into the smoke of the ship's hold a below-deck explosion occurred. Three firemen were badly burned and George McGregor later died of his injuries.

Apart from the much appreciated work of the London Fire Service Benevolent Fund, there was still much to be done to improve the new national conditions of service for firefighters. In October 1941 the Fire Brigades Union (FBU) was still campaigning for one standard wage for firemen instead of the "20 good, bad and indifferent" rates inherited from the various pre-NFS local authority fire brigades. The FBU also demanded that the government should pay full pay to any firefighters incapacitated through injury or sickness, instead of dismissing them at the end of 13 weeks if no recovery could be medically envisaged. In addition, the FBU sought a two-platoon (shift) duty system, fair and democratic promotion, and the abolition

A truly modern fire service was starting to emerge from the chaos and trauma of the Blitz period, but new terror weapons were on the horizon.

Another significant event was a gathering at Lambeth on 18 August, 1942 to mark the first year of the National Fire Service. After meeting firefighters from across No 5 Region, the Secretary of State for Home Affairs, Herbert Morrison MP, addressed the crews from a balcony and paid tribute to their sterling work.

61

of the penal clauses then prevalent in the discipline code.

By the summer of 1942 good progress had been made in standardizing and improving some of the more important aspects of the fire service. A national seven-volume training manual had been introduced, along with common uniforms, a rank structure and fire-ground control systems. A truly modern fire service was starting to emerge from the chaos and trauma of the Blitz period, but new terror weapons were on the horizon. They would bring death and carnage back to London and the southeast, and present the first serious operational challenges for the men and women of the NFS.

10 THE FUND GOES NATIONAL

…it was clear that the US donations should form the basis of a new national benevolent fund.

ALTHOUGH THE London Benevolent Fund was well established by the beginning of 1941, a number of other local benevolent and welfare aid funds in fire brigades of varying sizes still existed. In most cases these were generally organized by the larger city fire brigades – particularly those which had been hit by the *Luftwaffe*. Before the formation of the unified NFS, 1,635 individual fire brigades, large and small, provided the nation's fire cover and protection through the combined ranks of regular and AFS personnel.

It was the arrival during this period of the first donations from American and Canadian firefighters that acted as a catalyst and set the scene for the formation of a truly national benevolent fund for British firemen and women.

Soon after the first firefighter fatalities occurred during the early weeks of the London Blitz, an American organization known as the International Association of Firefighters (IAF), based in Washington, D.C., indicated that American firemen would like to collect dollars from their members for the direct benefit of the families of British firefighters. At the end of 1940 the Secretary of the IAF wrote to Major Jackson, London's fire chief, asking for guidance on how these US monies could best be put to immediate use.

Outside London, fire service casualties had continued to reflect the widespread nature of the air raids on other British cities, industrial centres and ports. As the London Benevolent Fund was working very efficiently within the new NFS uniformed framework, it was clear that the US donations should form the basis of a new national benevolent fund.

Ronnie Greene could clearly see that one all-embracing welfare fund to cover the overall needs of the British Fire Service should be created. He later wrote:

"Similar to the London Fund, there still existed a number of local fire brigade funds and their finances varied enormously. So too did their scales of grants. A fireman's widow in one place might get £5 when her husband was killed, whilst another widow in an adjacent geographical area got £25 or even £50. Payments seemed to depend upon the local conditions such as the density of population, size of town or city, and to some extent, the amount of Blitz raiding which those local firefighters had suffered.

Major Jackson therefore asked me to look at what would be involved in setting up another fund, entirely separate from the now successful London Fire Service Benevolent Fund, and one in no way linked to any existing local fire brigade fund elsewhere.

THE BENEVOLENT FUND

of the

NATIONAL FIRE SERVICE

1943

THE NATIONAL COUNCIL

WILL MEET ON

Tuesday, 17th August 1943, at Sixteen hours

AND

Wednesday, 18th August 1943, at Fifteen hours

PLACE OF MEETING

The County Hall, Westminster, London

Members are requested to bring this Volume with them.   It constitutes the Pass
on each occasion of entering or leaving the County Hall.

The cover of the historic programme for the inaugural meeting of the National Council which formally set up the new "national" Fund on 17 and 18 August, 1943.

63

64

The new Fund would specifically administer the American and other overseas donations. In September 1941, only one month after the National Fire Service came about, the National Fire Service Benevolent Trust was formed. It was named a **Trust** to ensure that it was distinct and not at all confused with the well-established London Fire Service Benevolent Fund organization.

The new NFS Trust was administered from the same offices at Southwark Bridge Road, London, SE1 by my small team who were already running the London Benevolent Fund. A great deal of all the work was done in our own time because we were all fully operational firemen and pretty busy ones too!

But the two organizations and their operations were kept quite separate. The London Fund was for London personnel and was controlled and supported by London firemen through their elected committees. The NFS Benevolent Trust was for **all** the fire service and administered on behalf of Chief Regional Fire Officers (CRFOs) of all the regions. Our job on their behalf was to distribute in the quickest possible manner the 'monies from America'.

At first, all the NFS Trust could manage to pay were basic death grants and orphans' allowances. We tried to be speedy and efficient and CRFOs soon came to realize how valuable it was in those hectic times to have a system of making a death grant by telegraph, usually within a very few hours of being notified of the death of a fireman or firewoman killed in action."

But there was a real concern in late 1941 that the American monies, which by then had totalled over £15,000, could not be expected to continue indefinitely. For one thing, the United States was under great pressure to join the Allied cause. More immediately worrying was the fact that the total grants and allowances paid by the NFS Trust started to exceed the UK income and the US dollars coming in. As Secretary of both the London Benevolent Fund and the NFS Trust, Ronnie Greene wrote:

"Some of us could see the end of the regular flow of the US and other overseas monies, and I think we had already shown something of what could be done with the NFS Benevolent Trust that one single national Benevolent Fund was not only highly desirable but morally essential to ensure fair treatment for all concerned."

On Tuesday 17 August, 1943 a two day meeting convened at County Hall, Westminster, London at which the National Fire Service Benevolent Fund was formally created.

Ronnie Greene's thoughts were prophetic. On Tuesday 17 August, 1943 a two day meeting was convened at County Hall, Westminster, London at which the National Fire Service Benevolent Fund was formally created. Its sole declared aim was to provide a single national body to provide welfare support to the nation's firefighters and their dependants.

The meeting was attended by 57 representatives from every NFS region and area, including Scotland and Wales, who would form the Fund's National Council. Right from the start the new body set out to be a truly democratic organization. Indeed, sitting side by side around the table at County Hall were a wide range of ranks from Leading Firemen to Fire Force Commanders.

Everyone at the National Council gathering echoed the need for one single fund.

High on the agenda was the appointment of the first Chairman of the Fund's National Council and Bailie Andrew Murray JP of the Scottish Home Department was duly elected. FD Sharples, a Column Officer from the Merseyside area who had been a lawyer prior to joining the AFS, was elected as the first Treasurer of the Fund. Not surprisingly, Ronnie Greene was also unanimously appointed as Honorary Organizing Secretary of the new national body. Both the Secretary of State for Home Affairs and the Secretary of State for Scotland accepted invitations to become the Fund's Honorary Presidents.

What was not widely realized at the time of that historic inaugural meeting was the enormous amount of time and effort which had preceded the first formal meeting of its National Council. Following governmental support during 1941 for a move towards a NFS welfare body, no fewer than 20 meetings had taken place between late 1941 and August 1943. Bailie Andrew Murray had chaired all of those preliminary meetings and Ronnie Greene had somehow found the time from his other duties to act as the secretariat.

Everyone at the National Council gathering echoed the need for one single fund. Some of the most important agreements reached at that historic meeting included an application to register the new Fund as a War Charity.

Furthermore, it was agreed to pool all existing finances of the various existing individual brigade schemes then in operation, including that of the London Benevolent Fund, into one central "kitty". Over a period of time the various local funds would be wound up.

At the inaugural meeting representatives presented a total sum of £29,200 from various NFS areas across the country. The London Fund undertook to continue to fund the death and orphans payments to London dependants until the National Fund was able to absorb this significant financial commitment. In addition, the new National Council also agreed to the provision of a standard range of death grants and allowances for its dependants.

These included a standard death benefit of £15, a payment of £4 in respect of each dependant orphan together with an orphan's weekly allowance of 4 shillings (20p) where the father's death was as a result of wartime action. Injury or sickness benefits were set at £2 per week for a maximum period of 75 weeks subject to local and national monitoring of individual cases. Hardship grants were also established whereby a one-off payment of £10 could be made. These benefits and grants would be administered by local committees formed of serving firemen and firewomen directly in touch with the needy cases concerned.

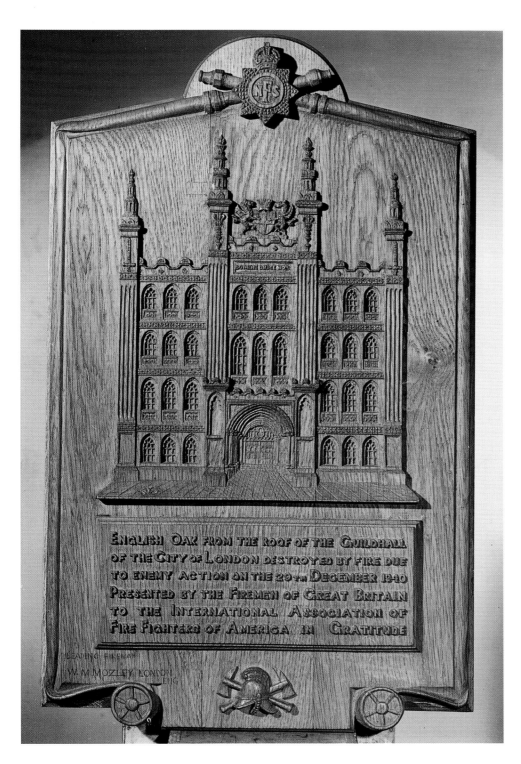

During her visit to Lambeth, Mrs Roosevelt was presented with a plaque to mark the generosity of American firefighters in helping the dependants of British crews who had died or been injured in the air raids of the past two years of war. This plaque was carved by Fireman William Mozley from an oak beam which had fallen from the roof of the Guildhall during the intense incendiary fire raid of 29 December, 1940.

Over the next few months the National Council would have much to consider and act upon, high on the priority list being many financial, legal, administrative and organizational issues involved in setting up an effective national network. But on that historic 17 and 18 August, 1943, the foundations of the modern day Fire Services National Benevolent Fund were truly born.

11 IN THE SERVICE OF THE NATION

COMMANDER AYLMER Firebrace was the pre-war chief of the London Fire Brigade. When war was declared in 1939 he was appointed Chief of the Fire Staff at the Home Office and Inspector in Chief of the Fire Service, in effect the government's principal advisor on firefighting matters.

Firebrace attended the inaugural meeting of the Council of the National Benevolent Fund in August 1943, and he was elected a Vice-President of the new Fund. He was particularly keen to make a personal contribution towards the new Fund and did so in a 16-page booklet which he wrote under the pseudonym "Centurion". Entitled *In the Service of the Nation*, the full colour booklet was published at cost for the Fund in October 1944 by the London publisher Raphael Tuck & Sons Ltd. *In the Service of the Nation* sold 50,000 copies within a few weeks of publication.

The booklet vividly described the way the NFS went into action when the bombs started to fall. With illustrations by London fireman artist Reginald Mills, this graphic work captured the danger of wartime firefighting and the spirit and selflessness of the firefighters. It is interesting to record that the final sales totals of *In the Service of the Nation* provided an income to the Fund of over £5,000.

In the following pages *In the Service of the Nation* is reproduced in its original 1944 form, complete with a brief foreword from the Fund's two inaugural Presidents, HM Secretary of State for Home Affairs, the Rt. Hon. Herbert Morrison MP, and HM Secretary of State for Scotland, the Rt. Hon. Thomas Johnston MP.

"In the Service of the Nation"

THE N·F·S GOES INTO ACTION

SCRIPT by "CENTURION"

PICTURED by FIREMAN REGINALD MILLS

PUBLISHED FOR THE
NATIONAL FIRE SERVICE BENEVOLENT FUND
(REGISTERED UNDER THE WAR CHARITIES ACT 1940)

By RAPHAEL TUCK & SONS LTD

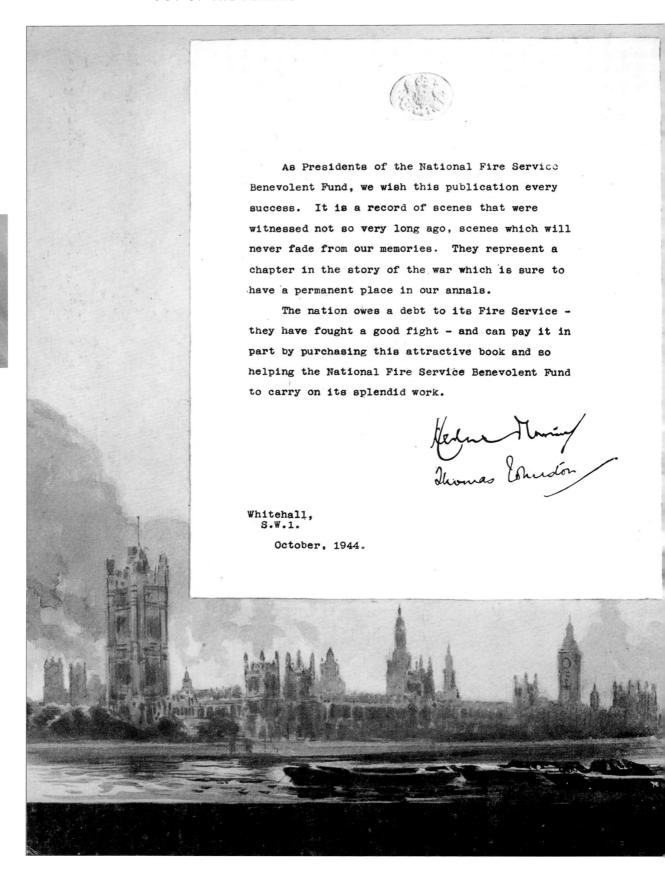

As Presidents of the National Fire Service Benevolent Fund, we wish this publication every success. It is a record of scenes that were witnessed not so very long ago, scenes which will never fade from our memories. They represent a chapter in the story of the war which is sure to have a permanent place in our annals.

The nation owes a debt to its Fire Service - they have fought a good fight - and can pay it in part by purchasing this attractive book and so helping the National Fire Service Benevolent Fund to carry on its splendid work.

Whitehall,
   S.W.1.

      October, 1944.

Observation Post

LL is quiet in Blanktown, and the local units of the N.F.S., who have been exercising late into the evening, have finished restowing their pumps and hose-laying lorries. Everything is blacked-out, and the dozen or so fire-stations in the town are settling down for the night; but in the control rooms N.F.S. women are awake and ready to take immediate action should a fire result, either from enemy action or just normal carelessness. But this will not be a quiet night—a group of enemy 'planes is heading for Blanktown. Listen! The sirens of this County Borough are even now sounding.*

Come with me into the principal fire-station. Here firemen are moving about, having a last look at their appliances; firewomen are stocking a canteen-van. The Divisional Officer pauses, surveying the scene.

'Any news, sir?'

'No, but it is just the sort of night that we might get something.'

He moves off and descends a stone staircase into an underground control room. Formerly used as a store, its ceiling is strutted against collapse with sizable timbers, and its walls are covered with maps and operational boards. A number of firewomen

---

* Though based on actual N.F.S. organisation, the incidents here described by a well-known Fire Service Officer are entirely fictitious.

Control room in action

" We've got a badly hurt man here"

and two men are present, and reports by telephone are coming through showing the state of readiness in the Division—how many pumps, special appliances, and officers are immediately available for action. Messages such as these will continue to come in for some time as N.F.S. part-timers report for duty at the call of the sirens, and so enable more and more pumps to be manned ready for action.

Now to an observation position on top of a high block of flats. The crew—two part-time women and an elderly part-time man, all in N.F.S. uniform—have uncovered their look-out shelter, seen their bearing plate in order, tested their telephone, which is a private wire to Divisional Control, and are now standing about, talking.

'Flares! Look!'

They're at their action stations in a flash. 'From No. 3 O.P.† : "Flares dropping in the dock area. Bearing 270. Barrage starting." '

Down in the Control Room the message is written out and handed, without comment, to the Mobilising Officer. A second message quickly follows : 'From No. 3 O.P.—" I.B.s falling between 260 and 270 near Brown's flour mills." '

The Mobilising Officer at once takes action, and, leaning over his message-pad, we see him write : 'Sub-Division 2—send 4 M.D.U.s to dock area to patrol for fires.' (An M.D.U. is a mobile dam unit, a fire appliance complete with pump and carrying its own supply of water.)

Fire calls from wardens and police are starting to come in, and pumps are being despatched to deal with them. Crump! . . . Crump! . . . Crump! Bombs fall a

† Observation position.

74

" There's a vast crater right across the road "

quarter of a mile away. Only one pump, a turn-table ladder, and a canteen-van now remain in the appliance room. The remaining fire-engines have either been dispersed to other stations, are out on a job, or are being parked at intervals round the drill yard. There's no point in having more than one appliance blown to bits at a time !

Appliance-room doors clatter open, and a car with a fire officer of Column rank, a woman driver at the wheel, goes out. We'll follow them.

The black-out is now broken by a number of fires, aircraft can be heard overhead, and noisy Ack-Ack guns are producing the effect of toy sparklers in the sky. The car pulls up at a group of fires. Four are attended, each by one appliance, but the top storeys of two private houses—one on each side of the road—are burning fiercely ; and meanwhile their owners stand in the street, gazing distractedly this way and that, hoping against hope that the N.F.S. will still arrive in time to save their homes, and maybe wishing that they had cleared their attics of rubbish and filled their baths with water. ' Oh ! Why don't they come ! ' But fire calls are now being received in stations as fast as telephone lines will carry them, and there are more fires burning than there are pumps in the town ; in any case, factories must receive priority over private houses—the war effort must have first consideration.

Nothing more to see here. We'll get back to the Divisional Control and take stock of the fire situation. Here entries as to fires and the movement of appliances are being chalked up on mobilising boards. The initiated can see, without asking a single question, how the fire situation stands. Twenty small fires, seven 5-pump fires, and one serious fire (a 25-pump job) at Nelson's factory—they make aircraft parts here, and so get a priority attendance of appliances. The N.F.S. is hard pressed—the board shows that there are many fires still waiting to be attended by the Fire Service. Twenty reinforcing pumps are on their way in from Whyford, but it will be half an hour before they can arrive.

The door of the Control Room opens and the Fire Force Commander enters. Tall, broad-shouldered, with an alert, cheerful face, he seems confident that the Fire Force, which he has subjected to intense training since Nationalisation, will give a good account of itself. As he runs his eye over the fire situation board, the Mobilising Officer steps to his side : ' Column Officer Brown's in charge of the Nelson's job, sir. I've asked for thirty additional pumps, and for another fifty to stand by. That ought to do us for the moment.'

' Good ! '

The Commander walks over to the Water Officer, who is studying a large-scale map. ' Water all right ? '

' All right so far as we know, sir. Two water units have gone to Nelson's to keep the static water-tanks there full. They are relaying up from the river—I've just come back from having a look at them.'

' Telephones all right ? '—it is now the turn of the Communications Officer (a company officer of some fifty years of age, he was once employed by the G.P.O.) to make his report.

' All lines in order except the private wire to Sub-Division 3—we're working on

Gas main alight

that. We've got two field-telephone vans standing by—one of them the women's crew—and a third is coming in from Zedborough. We've asked for ten more D.R.s‡ —we'll be very short if communications go !'

CRASH ! A violent earth tremor and at once darkness : a terrific blast of air has swept the Control Room, and there's a loud clatter as the door, blown off its hinges, strikes the floor. Message forms flutter to the ground.

A few exclamations ! A cry of ' Lights.' A calm ' Everyone all right ? ' from the Mobilising Officer—and in a minute or two things are normal again except that the lighting is now subdued—it comes from half a dozen hurricane-lamps—and the air is full of dust.

The Fire Force Commander is already half-way upstairs to the appliance room, where he finds that the next door building has been hit—and a cloud of thick black dust is rolling out from a vast heap of wreckage where once was a hotel. ' Tell 'em in the Control Room that the hotel's gone up, but the station's all right. Wardens are on the spot and will look after the job. Say I'm going to the Square.' A few seconds later and his car, followed by a despatch rider, is moving out of the station.

The raid is at its height. The barrage, at first spasmodic, is now almost continuous. Flares are still floating down undisturbed by the upward soaring red, green, and white tracer shells, though it is curious that they should still be used whilst serious fires in the centre of the town are illuminating a large area.

‡ Despatch Rider.

" Fires are spreading uncontrolled"

The Fire Force Commander speaks to his driver, without turning his head : ' They've found us to-night all right ! '

But she is too intent on her driving to reply, and at that moment the brakes screech, and the car bucks and jumps, finally coming to a standstill facing the way it had come—two yards from telephone wires festooned low across the road.

' Well done ! ' The driver does not answer, but the word of praise is not lost on her. ' Make for Anson Street.'

' Right, sir,'—and the car, turning round, mounts the pavement to dip under the wires at a point where they reach a higher level.

Brakes again ! A civilian has run into the road and held up the car. ' We've got a badly hurt man here—for God's sake take him to hospital ! '

' Sorry, I can't ! You can have my despatch rider, and he'll fetch an ambulance.' (It sounds callous, but firemen must not be diverted from their proper job—wounded are the concern of the ambulance service.)

The civilian, spattered with blood, is overwrought, and he tries to hold the car. ' Go on '—very firmly to the driver—and the man jumps cursing from the running-board as the car gathers speed.

Fifty yards from No. 3 Sub-Divisional Control, in Anson Street, the car stops—because it has to—there's a vast crater right across the road. It's a strange sight !

Fires were started

The fire-station itself is burning and so are the wooden palings on the opposite side of the road.

The Company Officer in charge is in his element—even cracking a joke with his subordinates. ' We'll get a new station out of this, anyway ! ' He comes over to the Fire Force Commander, who is scrambling round the edge of the crater. ' No water in this main, sir—I've sent the only two pumps I've got to relay from the canal. Telephones all gone ! I've sent a despatch rider to Divisional Control to tell 'em what's happened. The women are running a field-telephone line to the exchange.'

Take a look into the bottom of the crater. It's getting damp. Water is oozing through from a burst main, and now there is a cry from a fireman of ' Water ! ', and lo and behold, the crater fills rapidly. A pump is quickly man-handled into position, a long length of suction hose is lowered into the water, and the chance of getting a new fire-station vanishes as the fire in roof and top storey is brought under control.

But it's at the Square that things are looking worst. It's on fire on three sides— a scene of wild, evil beauty—and myriad sparks are driving furiously across the open space, stinging faces and making existence for the firemen, even those wearing special spark-trap goggles, extremely unpleasant. A number of hoses are laid out, but water is only passing through a few of them.

A Divisional Officer is in charge and he stands by the side of his Control Unit—an appliance of special design with conspicuous red-and-white chequer marking on each

Reinforcements on the way

side. Inside this mobile office—or advanced headquarters, call it what you will—a Section Leader is poring over a water-supply map. An N.F.S. typist taps her machine, entirely unconscious that it is unusual to do secretarial work by the light of burning buildings and to the noisy accompaniment of bombs, guns, and aeroplanes.

' To Division B—From Divisional Officer Thorne at the Square : " Make pumps 30 and turn-table ladders 3—Shortage of water, 1000 gallons per minute required—Send on 2 Column Officers and 4 Company Officers. Inform Fire Force Commander fires spreading, situation serious." '

She slips from her seat with the message and the Divisional Officer checks it. ' Good ! Well done ! ' He hands the message to the despatch rider : ' 'Way you go, Billings.' A kick at his starting lever, a gasping choke from the engine, another kick, and the D.R. is threading his way in and out of debris and unexploded bombs.

The fires are spreading uncontrolled, leaping viciously across one after another of the narrow streets leading off the Square. The few pumps at work are taking their water from steel dams, but these are rapidly being emptied. Plop, plop, plop !—and but fifty yards away from the pumps white flaming incendiary bombs are burning—in the roadway, on the pavements, two in the gutter close to a car. Presently one of these explodes with a deafening report and the car is a wreck.

The barrage continues, more violent and spectacular than ever, but the steady, growling, grunting throb of bombers overhead remains. They are concentrating on the fire area that they have created.

Here's an interesting sight. Look ! A hose-laying lorry, dashing into the Square at twenty miles per hour, laying out twin lines of $3\frac{1}{2}$-inch rubber-lined hose as it goes. It pulls up sharply, the crew jump out and take the goose-necked ends of their hoses to a circular steel dam. It seems an age to those waiting, while shops burn, flames leap and timbers crackle, before the hoses fill, curving snake-like under the pressure, and water flows splashing into the tank. But it doesn't remain there long, for trailer pumps, already set in, are playing it on to the fires.

Stop here and watch for a minute a group of firemen replacing a damaged length of 6-inch steel piping through which water has, until a bomb interfered, been passing up from the river to the centre of the town. What's that ? The men look up as a sharp roar is heard ! Machine-gunning ! Cannon fire ! They scatter, some flattening themselves against the base of a brick wall, others flinging themselves at full length along the gutter ; all cover their faces with their arms. A torrent of bullets rips up the asphalt road only a few yards from them, and spatters the wall, leaving it a pock-marked mass of crumbling red brick.

The firemen rise to their feet, obviously a bit shaken. One laughs nervously ; another swears softly to himself : ' The —— ——.' It was a very near thing for the whole party.

A steel water-tank across the way has been pierced by bullets in a dozen places, but firemen are handy men with an axe and soon plug the holes with pieces of wood.

Watch that 60-foot building—well alight on all floors ! Small pieces of cement and bits of the cornice stone are dropping, giving to the experienced fire-fighter warning of what is about to happen. Look at that crack widening in the front wall—

"RUN!"

Mobile Canteen

you can see right through it into the heart of the fire. The pumps' crews have seen it too—and the Section Leader in charge doesn't waste time or words. ' Water off ! Get out ! Run ! ' The pump is stopped, and, dropping their branch pipe, they start to run, just as the whole of the front of the building, pivoting at the first floor, crashes across the road. Fortunately for the pumps' crews, falling walls do not measure their full length—they break in mid-air. The wall has enveloped and battered into shape-lessness the pump and its equipment, but the crew, still running, are safe—by two yards ! They are cut and bruised by flying debris, but this they will not notice until later.

Turn round and see what is happening to this building on the opposite side of the Square—the hotel on the corner. A 100-foot turntable ladder is in use as a water tower—with a fireman (only a year ago he was a draper's assistant) swaying at the top, now directing water into the fire, and now wetting down the building next to it, so that it will not catch fire.

Do you hear that whistle ? This one's coming very close—it's fallen with a deafening explosion thirty feet from the corner ; nothing can be seen for smoke and dust. As it clears away, the chassis of the turn-table ladder can be seen lying twisted on its side. What's that lying on the roof of the cinema fifty yards to the right, projecting twenty feet over the street ? It's the 100-foot ladder, blown there by the explosion. And the crew ?—their next of kin will be informed in the morning. Strange that this ladder should be both built and destroyed by Germans !

Damping Down

It's a stiff fight for the N.F.S.   Where will they stop the fires ?   Will they stop them at all, or must they burn their way through to open spaces ?

Reinforcements are badly needed and they're on the way.   Along the country roads leading to the town, pumps and other appliances are coming at a smart pace, some in orderly convoy, some proceeding independently—most of them manned by part-timers, Britain's gallant fire-fighter reserve—all keen to get into action.   They will call at the N.F.S. reinforcement base on the outskirts of the town, opened up an hour ago with W.V.S. help.   Trailer pumps, with here and there a canteen-van, are arriving, and the Leading Firemen in charge are handing in their record papers, before being guided to the fires by messengers.   Six hours hence they will return here dog-tired, their faces black, their clothes sopping wet, and their appetites terrific.   That mobile kitchen—a gift from Canada—standing at the door once more will prove its usefulness, while its N.F.S. women crew, notwithstanding their loss of sleep and a hard night's work, will be feeling quietly satisfied at having come out on a worth-while job.

The sirens are now sounding the ' All Clear.'   The fire-fighters make no comment— they're almost too tired now even to speak, but they feel a sense of relief.   Bombing and machine-gunning are over—that's something.   Fires are coming under control, now that reinforcements are at work, but there's a lot to be done yet.   The firemen brighten up as a canteen-van, manned by two N.F.S. girls in skiing type slacks, arrives and opens up.   Many of the firemen they know, and there is a rapid exchange of raid gossip.

' Brooks's has gone, and Wellman's is burnt out ; the Arcade's on fire, but they've got the stop for it.   A2's had all its windows blown out, but no one hurt.'   And so on.

Presently the canteen will move to the next fire, and the next, and the next—then back for fresh supplies and out again.   The firemen continue with their jobs, some rolling up hose, some damping down the still smouldering fires and attending to bulls eyes § ; others are placing ramps in position over the hose, protecting it from the traffic.

These men are almost ' out on their feet '—utterly exhausting work, fire-fighting, and they've had eight hours of it.   But they wouldn't have missed it for anything— the National Fire Service welcomes the chance of going into action.

§ Glowing pieces of wood in ceilings and beams which have so far escaped the water from the branches.

NATIONAL · FIRE · SERVICE

Script by kind permission of "Chambers's Journal"

FIREWOMEN!

THE dismal note of a siren warbles its message drear,
And its equally dismal fellows chorus it far and near;
The women of the N.F.S. maintain their watch and ward,
Manning communication lines against the Hunnish horde.

"Forty-eight on and twenty-four off" the women's hours are long,
Their training must be thorough and their courage must be strong,
For *if* they were to falter, the fire defence would fail
And flames would rage unhindered, leaving ruin in their trail.

Distant rumble of gunfire, tracers and flares in the sky,
A growing sense of tension as the evening's raid draws nigh.
The station cat's uneasy and drops from a friendly lap,
Then, crouching, waits for the whistle of bomb, dreading its thunder-clap.

The tension breaks with the start of fires; there's more than enough to do,
For the fires are very many and the pumps are very few;
An urgent hum of voices pervades the busy hive,
Reports of water shortage and of pumps that *won't* arrive.

Both sides of the street now burning, office and shop aflame,
But the "Women at War" don't bother, it's all a part of the game;
Excited cry from a warden—"Your b—y roof's alight!"
The answer they give is flippant; and he's gone into the night.

The building rocks, the lights go out, there's a moment of deadly fear,
Outside . . . a yawning crater—inside . . . a nervous cheer;
Oil lamps are lit on the instant and a sigh of relief is heard,
The N.F.S. control room staff continues undeterred.

The heat is overpow'ring, there's a growling bomber din,
Their chance of escape grows slender as the angry fires close in.
When every "line's" reported "dead" and it's suicide to stay,
The order comes, "Abandon ship!"—"to fight another day!"

They gasp as they reach the open; it's an awe-inspiring scene,
Of raging fires and ruin, where a city once had been.
The streets are piled with debris; there are firemen lying dead;
A stinging hail of fiery sparks; and red clouds overhead.

＊　　＊　　＊　　＊

In dogged mood the N.F.S. awaits each night's alarms,
Its men and women glory in the comradeship of arms,
They've still their sense of humour, their ardour does not tire
In the Service of the Nation for the Mastery of Fire.

Script by kind permission of "Chambers's Journal"

A child is rescued and
carried to safety from the
rubble and destruction of
yet another enemy raid.

12 HORROR WEAPONS

Opposite: The new horror weapon arrives. A V1 has just fallen in Middlesex Street in London, E1. Firemen, civil defence workers and police begin the search for survivors. (London Fire Brigade)

AFTER THE formation of the NFS in August 1941, bombing raids continued on both London and the provinces although not at the pace and intensity of the attacks earlier in the war. Indeed, during 1942-43, there were only 28 serious air raids in the London area. However, the London region did send significant firefighting support convoys to other areas during the many "Baedeker" raids in the spring of 1942. They were christened "Baedeker" because Hitler had promised that he would raze every British town and city that appeared in that well-known guide-book. These raids hit Norwich, Reading, Exeter, Bristol, Bath, Oxford and Taunton. Later attacks struck Canterbury, Peterborough and Birmingham.

Soon there were few parts of England where firefighters had not experienced a bomb attack of some sort or other. The good news was that, after a few teething troubles, by summer 1942 the NFS organization had settled down well to its task. By then the NFS boasted a national strength of over 55,000 men and women, and much needed consolidation of equipment and training procedures was already under way. The NFS was never likely to be as severely tested by fire as London and several other brigades had been in the 1940/41 Blitz period. The improved organization showed in the way that the many convoys during the "Baedeker" raids worked

*Soon there were few parts of England where firefighters
had not experienced a bomb attack of some sort or other.*

The audible warning of a V1's approach underlined the value of permanently manned NFS observation posts at the top of fire station drill towers. They were able to spot and locate promptly the many V1 explosions.

much more smoothly and without experiencing the many problems of the past.

But a new challenge for the NFS was looming. On 13 June, 1944 an alert sounded in east London at 0350hrs. It was to signal a new and deadly phase of the war on the home front. Searchlights picked up a plane which was soon downed by intense anti-aircraft fire. Four minutes later, the NFS received a call to inspect a crashed aircraft on open ground near Barking. The burning wreckage appeared to be that of a small aircraft but even as the crews were dealing with the fire, another similar alert in East London was sounding. An NFS officer recalled:

"But instead of the expected quiet which usually follows, a loud sound was heard which I attributed to a single engine plane in a power dive. The sound of the engine continued for what I thought would be an extraordinarily long dive and as my thoughts flashed to a plane which might have been hit or which was in trouble, the engine sound abruptly ceased. There was silence for a few seconds, followed by a violent explosion which shook the whole neighbourhood."

The crash and explosion demolished several terraced houses and there was extensive damage all around. Along with the Civil Defence services, the NFS went to work to extinguish a few small fires, and extricate the dead and injured from collapsed buildings. What had caused this carnage? Many said it was an aircraft but no bodies of airmen were recovered. It soon emerged that the explosions were caused by an unmanned flying projectile.

By the end of that week of June, 44 similar incidents had been reported in London and the south-east. All were attended by the NFS. Careful inspection of the wreckage confirmed that Hitler's new terror weapon was a pilotless flying bomb, known as the V1. Powered by a ramjet petrol-injection engine, it carried 2,200lb (1,000kg) of high explosive. The V1s were launched from sites in France and Holland and flew at 350mph (560kph) before the engine cut out. The V1 then dived silently for about a minute before crashing into its target area with a huge detonation of its lethal charge. The V1s were the world's first cruise missiles.

The audible warning of a V1's approach underlined the value of permanently manned NFS observation posts at the top of fire station drill towers. They were able to spot and locate promptly the many V1 explosions.

The first attack heralded one of the busiest times for NFS crews in the London area. 638 V1s fell in June 1944 alone, and although a V1 explosion did not always cause fire, there was plenty of rescue work and assistance for the many

casualties needed, as well as the sad task of the recovery of any fatalities from under the tons of rubble of collapsed buildings. In July 1944 1,121 V1s fell to ground. On 2 July alone 80 V1s dropped out of the sky. The most frantic day was 3 August, when 97 V1 incidents were logged in the London region, presenting London crews with one of their most dangerous and challenging days since the September 1940 Blitz.

Some of the fires which were started were a fire-raiser's heaven. On 2 July, 1944 a V1 fell right into the centre of a riverside candle factory in Bermondsey. The building was full of barrels of paraffin wax, contained 60 tons (61 tonnes) of fuel oil, and 2,000 gallons (9,100 litres) of turpentine. All the barges moored alongside the factory wharf were full of paraffin wax and part of the surface of the Thames was soon alight.

Another V1 struck a gasometer near Kennington Oval, while another fell into a tar works. Here firemen were confronted with a burning river of tar slowly advancing towards them, like a creeping lava flow from an erupting volcano. And amid all this fiery hell, there were plenty of challenging and difficult rescues of trapped casualties to be carried out. Working in conjunction with the Civil Defence Heavy Rescue teams, firemen had to dig into cavities in compacted debris when a casualty could be heard crying out for help, or where it was believed persons had been buried in the V1 explosion.

There were some amazing escapes from this phase of the Blitz. This woman is fully conscious as firemen carefully extricate her from the debris of her house in Whitta Road, Manor Park, East London, October 1944. (London Fire Brigade)

Worse was to come. On 9 September, 1944 the second phase of the horror-weapon attacks started when the first V2 rocket fell on the civilian population of London. The V2 was an even more deadly weapon of war than the V1, which at least gave some warning of its approach. The V2 was the first true military ballistic missile. It carried one tonne of high explosive and was fired on a high trajectory at considerable speed. There was no warning of its approach; the first evidence of its arrival was a huge and devastating explosion. Whereas a V1 would demolish several houses, a V2 destroyed a whole street.

From September 1944 V2 rockets fell regularly causing great injury and loss of life and immense damage to housing and commercial buildings. The intensity of the V2 attacks reached a pitch in February 1945, with 115 falling on the London area in that month alone. Some idea of the carnage caused by a V2 rocket can be gained from the casualty figures of just two incidents. In November 1944 a V2 struck a block of flats in New Cross, south London killing 268 men, women and children. Another V2 attack at lunchtime on an office block near Moorgate in the City of London left 233 men and women office staff dead and hundreds injured.

However, following the D-Day invasion of Normandy in June 1944, the Allies advanced across northern France and, even though the V2 was fired from mobile launchers, the Germans progressively had to pull back their V1 and V2 launching sites. On 27 March, 1945 the last V1 and V2 fell on British soil near Orpington in Kent. A total of 2,381 V1 flying bombs and 511 V2 rockets had fallen on the Greater London area in the course of the barrage.

For the NFS, this marked the end of the fire service's war on the Home Front. However, an overseas NFS column had been formed in readiness to follow the invading troops into enemy-occupied territory, for there was a real fear of an enemy fire-blitzkrieg as the German forces retreated. In the event, it was not necessary to mobilize the overseas column across the Channel.

Peace finally came to Europe on 8 May, 1945. Over 1,000 British firefighters had been killed in action, including 393 in the London region. Over 7,000 were seriously injured. Of London's 875 fire stations, no fewer that 662 had been damaged by fire or bomb blast. More than 50,000 separate wartime fire and rescue incidents had been attended.

The gallantry of firefighters was duly recognized by many awards. The George Cross was awarded to Auxiliary Fireman Errington for his rescue of colleagues trapped in the burning basement of their fire station in central London on 17 September, 1940. Badly burned during his gallant rescue effort, Errington

*The V2 was the first true military ballistic missile.
It carried one tonne of high explosive and was fired on a
high trajectory at considerable speed. There was no
warning of its approach; the first evidence of its arrival
was a huge and devastating explosion.*

suffered the indignity of being compulsorily discharged from the service when his burns failed to heal within the 13-week period. The London Benevolent Fund was able to swing into action to assist in his recovery.

Other major gallantry awards to fire service personnel included 38 George Medals, including one to Auxiliary Firewomen Tanner for extreme coolness and courage shown during the night raid of 20 September, 1940 when she volunteered to drive a van loaded with five-gallon (23-litre) jerrycans of petrol to refuel the many pumps at work in central London streets while incendiary and high explosive bombs were still falling. 152 other members of the London Fire Brigade, the London Auxiliary Fire Service and, latterly, the NFS were commended for acts of bravery carried out under extreme enemy action.

The V2 rockets caused even more widespread damage, death and injury. This scene captures the drama in early 1945 soon after V2 attacks began with firemen and others carrying injured children to safety.

13 PEACE AND REORGANIZATION

BY THE time that peace in Europe was finally declared, the National Fire Service Benevolent Fund was well established throughout the British fire service via a nationwide network. The mainstay of the Fund then – as it is today – was the station representative who was elected by his or her colleagues. This person's role was to keep in touch with people whom the Fund sought to help, hopefully to inspire others to promote fund-raising functions and events, and to represent the fire station on the local Fund committee, perhaps even to serve as an elected member of the National Council. Right from its inception, Ronnie Greene insisted that the Fund should be run on democratic lines. No regard was paid to length of service or rank. There was never a membership as such, no entrance fees, dues or subscriptions; benefits were available for all.

The National Council continued to administer the growing income of the Fund and dealt with the demand for any help which the Fund could provide for widows, orphans, and uniformed personnel in need of support of various kinds. In 1945, there were 1,364 orphans on the Fund's register and the National Council was able to announce an increase of two shillings (10p) in the orphan's allowance to a total of of six shillings (30p) per week.

The annual report of the Executive Committee to the National Council spoke of "…the Fund's unqualified progress and achievement in excess of even the most optimistic anticipations of a year ago". Another section of the annual report noted:

> "Despite the difficulties imposed by his onerous operational responsibilities, our Honorary Secretary, Ronnie Greene, with his loyal and efficient staff have not only met the heavy burden of day-to-day requirements of the regions and areas, but he has initiated and organized with marked success a number of national schemes for gathering monies and publicizing the work of the Fund. It is impossible to express appreciation to Ronnie Greene and his assistant, Mr Jenkins, in anything like adequate terms."

Ronnie Greene and his small team, now based in offices over Shoreditch fire station in Tabernacle Street, London, EC2, were very busy with the development of the Fund. Despite trying to keep the structure of the National Fund at a simple level, it had been necessary to set up various sub-committees to look after different aspects of the Fund's growing work. In this task the assistance of various professional, legal and financial advisors, often seconded from the civilian staff of the larger pre-war fire

Ronnie Greene insisted that the Fund should be run on democratic lines. No regard was paid to length of service or rank. There was never a membership as such, no entrance fees, dues or subscriptions.

A group of NFS firemen from the London area are captured by the camera during a weekend training exercise in the spring of 1945. Although the end of hostilities is in sight, many of these firefighters have endured the horrors and suffering of the London Blitz and they were all, no doubt, looking forward to happier times ahead.

brigades, was invaluable. In 1945 these sub-committees included those dealing with Finance, Appeals and Publicity, Future Constitution, Post-War Planning, and Orphans' Allowances.

Income and donations to the Fund for the year to December 1945 totalled £189,782 – a truly staggering amount considering that only £29,110 was raised in 1943-44, the first full year of the National Fund. Some of this income had been raised by differing appeals and schemes, such as a BBC radio broadcast on the "Week's Good Cause" series (£1,562); a National Savings Stamp Poster scheme (£4,231), and Flag Days organized locally by firefighters at various fire stations (£3,000). Ronnie Greene also arranged for a pictorial exhibition to be staged in a London department store that set out the work of the fire service during the Blitz and the V1 and V2 attacks. This alone raised over £4,000 during a two-week period.

This exhibition included work created by a number of London firemen and

98

firewomen who had been professional artists before the outbreak of war. Encouraged by London's regular officers, this small band used their off-duty time to produce striking representations in oils, watercolour and pencil sketches of dramatic scenes from the Blitz. So high was the standard that four exhibitions were staged between 1941-44 at the Royal Academy in London, and later in other parts of the United Kingdom. Two collections drawn from the work of these fire service artists were also sent to the United States and Canada. Much of the proceeds of this activity eventually-found its way into the coffers of the Benevolent Fund.

In 1945, as far as the Fund's income generated by firefighters themselves was concerned, the Regions which embraced the larger cities naturally performed most impressively, simply due to the large numbers of personnel who became involved in fund-raising. The NFS North Midland (Region 3) recorded the largest single donation of £10,000. Personnel in Region 9 (West Midlands) topped the year's list of collective fund-raising with £27,722, including £5,000 raised in one week. In the rural areas of the NFS, there were also some impressive efforts. Fire crews from Haverfordwest fire station formed an amateur dramatic company which performed

The Fund was committed to improving the levels of grants and allowances to widows and orphans, and to other needy cases caused by injury or sickness.

A small group of the Fund's National Council members stand respectfully at the Fire Service section of the annual Field of Remembrance outside Westminster Abbey in November 1949. Left to right: Chief Fire Officer KN Hoare, Manchester (Chairman of the Fund); CV Bentley, Bolton (Vice Chairman); EE Holloway, Liverpool (Assistant Treasurer); Mrs BW Cuthbert CBE (Vice-President); J Camp, West Ham; J Berry, West Riding of Yorkshire; AB Robertson, London; H Williams BEM, Flintshire; and DC Mitchell, Glamorgan.

99

shows in the West Wales area during the summer and autumn of 1944. Over £800 was raised for the Fund.

Apart from the many specific and varied national fund-raising events organized within the service, donations from the public continued to flow in. A report to the regular Fund's National Council during this time spoke of:

"…the infinitely encouraging and small sums subscribed with accompanying letters from widows, OAPs, and persons of slender means, all of whom from the richness of their hearts and association with the work of the fire service felt they wanted to donate."

The Fund was committed to improving the levels of grants and allowances to widows and orphans, and to other needy cases caused by injury or sickness. In the early days, this was still the main practical aid that the Fund was able to provide. A total of £38,000 was spent in this way in 1944-45, although the improving income situation also

For the Benevolent Fund, it continued to be a time of challenge, development and not a little financial anxiety as the need grew to keep the level of income and donations abreast of the ever-growing expenditure...

On 3 January, 1950 the London Fire Brigade organized a children's party at Lambeth HQ for the families of some of the Fund's 1,467 widows. During the party the children were entertained by magicians, a Punch and Judy show, cartoon films, and then they enjoyed a special tea. During the afternoon Australian and New Zealand government representatives distributed food parcels. Here some of the children enjoy the magic show.

meant that new and welcome developments could be implemented.

One of these was the provision of motorized wheelchairs for former firefighters who had suffered injuries leading to permanently disability. Five such wheelchairs were presented by the Fund to disabled firemen during 1944-45. This was the start of a scheme to provide mobility for disabled former members which has continued to the present day. One of the first of these motorized wheelchairs was presented to Fred Munson, a London AFS fireman who had been badly injured in March 1941 at a fire in Millwall. Fred was paralysed from the waist down after being trapped when part of a burning building col-

lapsed on him. He was discharged from the NFS on 24 October, 1941 and spent the next few years in and out of hospital receiving surgery and treatment to his injuries. Fred Munson proved himself a stalwart character, showing both forbearance in putting up with his disability and being a tremendous ambassador for the Benevolent Fund and its work.

Another significant improvement which the Fund was able to implement in 1947 was to increase the widow's death grant to £100. During the early months of that year, the uniformed part of the British Fire Service was preparing for another major upheaval. As the country slowly got back on its feet after the war years, the government prepared

During the party, the children noisily greet the arrival of Father Christmas from the vantage point of Lambeth's turntable ladder.

101

to return control of the fire service to the local authorities.

After months of planning, meetings and political consultations, followed by a Parliamentary Bill, the Fire Services Act 1947 became effective on 1 April, 1948. From that date, the NFS was no more. 147 "new" fire brigades were established and they were to be the direct legal responsibility of metropolitan cities, county councils and county boroughs. Thus the government fulfilled a promise made to local authorities upon the hurried creation of the NFS back in 1941. It was the end of a dramatic era and the beginning of a new one which would consolidate all the hard lessons of fire-fighting and rescue work learned during the war years.

For the Fire Services National Benevolent Fund, it continued to be a time of challenge, development and not a little financial anxiety as the need grew to keep the level of income and donations abreast of the ever-growing expenditure on grants, allowances and the costs of a range of general assistance and aid provided.

14 STEADY GROWTH

Opposite: During 1950 the Fund was able to send a number of firefighters suffering from tuberculosis to a specialist clinic at Leysin in Switzerland where a complete cure could be effected over a three-month stay. This is the clinic and sanatorium in the mountains near Leysin where the British firemen were successfully treated. The Fund met all the costs of this revolutionary medical care which was unavailable on the infant National Health Service.

WHEN THE government announced its intention to wind up the National Fire Service and return the responsibility for the nation's fire service to local authorities on 1 April, 1948, the Fund's National Council agreed to various changes to the Fund's constitution necessitated by the de-nationalization of the fire service. Among these was an agreement that the Fund's title should be changed from The National Fire Service Benevolent Fund to the Fire Services National Benevolent Fund (FSNBF) to reflect its new peacetime status.

The approach of the 1950s heralded a period of steady growth and consolidation. One of the Fund's guiding principles, one which still applies today, was to increase and widen the scope of its activities whenever its financial position permitted. With fund-raising and income growing steadily through a wide range of events involving fire stations across the British fire service, a number of developments could be implemented.

When the fire service returned to local authority control in 1948, its total uniformed strength was many times greater than the country required for its peacetime fire defence. As a result, many men and women who had joined the AFS during the war years were released to return to civilian life. In order to reflect the immeasurable work and sacrifice of the nation's wartime firefighters, the Fund's National Council agreed to allow retired or former members of both the AFS (1938-1941) and NFS (1941-1948) to continue to be eligible for the full benefits of the FSNBF.

One of those who retired was Ronnie Greene, the Fund's Honorary Secretary and driving force, who had risen to the rank of Assistant Fire Force Commander in the London region of the NFS by the end of the war. Though nominally retired, Ronnie continued to devote most of his time to the development of the Fund; he was also able to begin the post-war commercial regeneration of Wimbledon Speedway.

As the new peacetime fire service settled down to fresh challenges and a growing operational workload, Ronnie Greene, together with his small secretarial staff, moved from accommodation above Shoreditch Fire Station to an office in 94 Southwark Bridge Road, adjacent to the London Fire Brigade Training Centre. Interestingly, it was the same office in which the London Fire Service Benevolent Fund had seen the light of day back in the dramatic early days of the London Blitz in September 1940. This accommodation was made available on a lease from the Brigade.

In 1945, soon after the Fund's offices were relocated to an office above Shoreditch Fire Station, a second-hand clothing store had been opened there in a spare storeroom. Despite the move back to Southwark, the much-appreciat-

One of the Fund's guiding principles, one which still applies today, was to increase and widen the scope of its activities whenever its financial position permitted.

The first British firefighter to attend the Leysin TB clinic in 1950 was Station Officer Harry Thorpe of Bolton Fire Brigade. After his stay high in the bracing mountain air, the rejuvenated officer smiles at the camera before boarding the mountain railway for the journey back home and to his job in the fire service.

ed clothing facility remained available at Shoreditch to members until it was finally closed in 1951.

The post-war Fund also embraced the thousands of volunteer or "retained" firefighters who were now serving throughout the rural county fire brigades. After basic training, these volunteer firefighters pursued their normal occupations and leisure activities until a 999 call came in day or night. Then they would dash to the fire station to man the fire engine and respond to the fire or other emergency. For this commitment, these volunteers were paid an annual bounty together with an attendance fee.

After the war, the "retained" service made up about half of the total fire cover in Great Britain and it was important for the FSNBF to recognize their work and commitment. After all, these volunteers potentially faced the same dangers and personal risks as professional firefighters. Alongside all retained firefighters, the firemen of industrial works' fire brigades were also brought within the scope of the Fund.

Recognizing the potential pressure on the Fund's resources, at one of its regular meetings in 1950, the Executive Committee of the FSNBF decreed that the Fund's priorities should be:

Quite a significant number of firefighters affected by TB were faced with the likelihood of forced retirement from the uniformed fire service.

1 Help for orphans.
2 Help for the injured or disabled.
3 Help for dependants (other than orphans) of those killed on duty or who died as a direct result of sickness or injury which was the cause of their discharge from the service.
4 Help for members or former members of the service to alleviate hardship directly attributable to service as a firefighter.

During 1950, a remarkable new scheme was introduced by the Fund. During the immediate post-war period, there had been a significant increase in the incidence of pulmonary tuberculosis (TB) amongst the population. There was a long waiting list for treatment in the United Kingdom for the many people who were seriously ill, but deemed to be curable. Quite a significant number of firefighters affected by TB were faced with the likelihood of forced retirement from the uniformed fire service. As a result, the National Council of the Fund agreed to introduce a pilot scheme offering TB cure at a sanatorium in Leysin, Switzerland. The first serving fireman to travel to Switzerland was Station Officer Harry Thorpe of Bolton Fire Brigade. He went to Leysin in September 1950 and, after a three-month stay, came back to his brigade completely cured. Over the next two years, 20 other British firemen underwent successful treatment in Switzerland, with all expenses being met by the Fund.

By 1951, the Fund's income had grown sufficiently to allow the orphan's weekly allowance to be increased to six shillings per week. In that year there were almost 1,400 children on the Fund's orphan list. One particular addition to the Fund's benefits was welcomed by these young dependants. With the help of Fund representatives from brigades in seaside areas, Ronnie Greene was able to organize free summer holidays for many of its children. The Fund paid the travelling expenses and allowed each child ten shillings pocket money. Over 450 separate holiday schemes for orphans were staged during the summer of 1951.

1951 also saw the development of a "new" Auxiliary Fire Service (AFS) created by the government, primarily to assist public fire brigades to meet the growing threat of conflict on the home front which might involve atomic weapons. The new AFS was progressively built up in the early 1950s and was equipped by the Home Office with new Bedford fire engines painted in dark green livery. They were quickly dubbed "Green Goddesses". The post-war AFS continued to be maintained until 1968. Its uniformed men and women were all treated as full members of the FSNBF.

As the work of the Fund grew, the National Executive Committee issued a booklet containing guidance for local

During the 1950s, there was probably not a fire station in the country that was not contributing to fund-raising in some way and supporting the growing work of the FSNBF. Here a young boy cannot resist ringing the bell of the toy fire-engine collecting box outside a fire station of Newcastle and Gateshead Fire Brigade.

representatives, which set out a standard format for dealing with dependants and their needs, the range of grants and allowances, and other procedural issues. These administrative arrangements were ground-breaking, and gave a certain level of autonomy to local committees. At that time, such devolution was not employed by any other national charity. Although experimental then, the arrangements have stood the test of time well, and – regularly updated – are still in use today.

One of the most significant events during this period came in 1953 when Her Majesty The Queen agreed to become the Patron of the Fire Services National Benevolent Fund. There is no doubt that this Royal accolade truly recognized the far-reaching work of the Fund during its first decade of existence, and reflected the hard work and enthusi-

One of the most significant events during this period came in 1953 when Her Majesty The Queen agreed to become the Patron of the Fire Services National Benevolent Fund.

asm of officers and local representatives right across the structure of the British fire service.

Much of the work leading up to granting of Royal patronage was carried out by CV Bentley, Chief Fire Officer of Bolton Fire Brigade and FSNBF Chairman 1951-53, together with the Fund's Honorary Solicitor, J Tindal-Robertson, who had succeeded Howard Roberts in 1949.

Although the FSNBF had a small investment portfolio, most of its income derived from fund-raising activities carried on at fire stations up and down the country. Without exception, most of this effort was put in during off-duty time. Flag days were an important part of the work, and various local initiatives produced a steady flow of income. These included jumble sales, raffles, sports days, and garden fêtes.

Some events were more ambitious. These included an inaugural concert staged jointly by the Northampton and Northamptonshire Fund representatives. Held at the Granada cinema in Kettering on 25 November, 1951, it featured the Luton Girls Choir. It was such a success that for some years the event became a major annual gathering in the county. In 1954, the concert was held in Northampton. Apart from the girl's choir, it also featured the Central Band of the RAF. One year later it played host to the Band of the Irish Guards.

Not to be outdone, the Fund's organizers in neighbouring Buckinghamshire Fire Brigade put on a very successful Olde Tyme Ball at High Wycombe in April 1955 at which Sydney Thompson's BBC Orchestra performed.

Through the 1950s the success of all this activity was reflected in the FSNBF annual fund-raising income figures (as shown below). The growing demands and annual costs of the Fund's services clearly illustrate how vital it was for the annual income stream to be maintained:

	Income £	Expenditure £
1954	46,350	42,200
1956	56,800	53,760
1958	60,050	48,750
1960	106,770	67,270

As the end of the decade approached, it was evident to Ronnie Greene and a few others that if the Fund's financial resources continued to grow at an equivalent rate, the National Council should seriously consider the acquisition of some property to help convalescent patients or for a similar use by the Fund's dependants. In 1961, the quest for a suitable property began in earnest. This exercise would launch the FSNBF into a new chapter in its progressive development and was to become the springboard for a widening of the provision of benefits for the men and women of the British fire service.

15 LANDMARKS AT LITTLEHAMPTON

IT WAS in 1960 at a meeting of the National Executive Committee (NEC) that Ronnie Greene first raised the question of buying a suitable property for convalescent use by injured firefighters and their families. At first the idea received a very cool response but eventually Ronnie did manage to gather sufficient support to start a search for a modest property situated in a suitably quiet location. But it was not an easy task. House prices were rising steadily and the available finances within the Fund were constantly being earmarked to improve and develop existing grants and allowances.

Two particular benefit improvements introduced in 1961 included a regular grant to widows of 10 shillings per week, and the first education grants to orphans to allow them to pursue higher education courses through to first-degree graduation from university. But in 1961 the medium-term financial future of the Fund was sufficiently worrying for then Chairman, Chief Fire Officer John Fordham of Kent, to write an open letter to all British firefighters:

"…I appeal personally on behalf of the Benevolent Fund's forthcoming Christmas stocking campaign. The Fund's revenue has dropped alarmingly compared to the same period twelve months ago, but grants are ever increasing."

House prices were rising steadily and the available finances within the Fund were constantly being earmarked to improve and develop existing grants and allowances.

Purchased in 1964, Marine Court in Fitzalan Road, Littlehampton, West Sussex, consisted of 12 flats in this new residential block, the first convalescent accommodation owned by the Fund. Ronnie Greene's office was also located in Marine Court. It was the first permanent administration base of the FSNBF. Within two years, the remainder of the block had been acquired to extend the provision of convalescent care.

109

Fortunately, CFO Fordham's words must have helped. Thanks to the continuing efforts of local representatives and firefighters serving at many fire stations across the country, by the end of 1962 total income had risen to a new record of £105,624. Flag days contributed £10,290 to this magnificent total, while fire-engine collecting boxes in retail shops and other locations raised £5,859. Sadly, during the year, seven firemen were killed in operational action and six orphans were added to the register.

While this fund-raising effort was going on, Ronnie Greene, now working from a temporary Fund Head Office in Altyre Road, Croydon, kept quietly working away at the idea of providing a proper convalescent home. At that time, Ronnie and his wife Maureen were planning to have a new house built in Littlehampton in West Sussex. They had kept a small boat in the harbour there for some years and the sunny location of the town close to a long sandy seafront seemed ideal for a convalescent home. Mindful of the rising cost of seaside property, Ronnie first floated the idea of purchasing some caravans on a permanent site during a meeting of the Fund's governing NEC. This suggestion was not well received, but, undaunted, Ronnie continued to argue the case for the Fund to acquire its first permanent property. At meetings of both the Executive Committee and National Council, his idea was minuted as the "Convalescent Scheme". Over a period of months, the Honorary Organizing Secretary worked slowly at convincing members of the NEC that the acquisition of a property portfolio would be a positive step for the Fund.

There remained resistance to the idea of buying caravans, but the feeling started to emerge, within both the NEC and National Council, that bricks and mortar might be a better investment. Ronnie wasted no time. He arranged for a number of properties in Littlehampton to be viewed along with some houses in other seaside towns including Herne Bay, in Kent, Skegness in Lincolnshire, and Scarborough in North Yorkshire. But it was still hard to get a clear consensus from the NEC. Some felt the whole idea was foolhardy; others took the view that the price of most suitable large houses was well beyond the Fund's means at that time. Another difficulty was that even amongst those who did support Ronnie Greene's view, there appeared to be no ready agreement about whether the Fund should decide on a northerly or a southerly location for any convalescent home.

Some compromise seemed necessary. But it was not until the weekend that Ronnie and Maureen Greene visited the show flat of a newly completed block of 24 self-contained residential flats called Furzedown Court in Fitzalan

Over a period of months, the Honorary Organizing Secretary worked slowly at convincing members of the NEC that the acquisition of a property portfolio would be a positive step for the Fund.

Don Bates, Chairman of the FSNBF and Chief Fire Officer of Glamorgan Fire Service, makes a welcoming speech to guests at the official opening of Marine Court on 13 May, 1965.

111

Marine Court at Littlehampton was opened as the FSNBF's first convalescent centre in September 1964. Each of the flats had two bedrooms, a reception room, fully fitted kitchen and bathroom and toilet, and was centrally heated.

112

One of the Fund's VIP guests at the official opening of Marine Court was wartime London AFS fireman Fred Munson. Fred, who was badly injured in the collapse of a building during a Blitz raid in 1941, had been one of the first disabled members of the Fund. After the war he worked tirelessly to raise money and promote the work of the Fund. Here Fred is greeted by Ronnie Greene and Don Bates.

Road, close to the seafront at Littlehampton, that events started to accelerate. They had visited Furzedown Court looking for general ideas for their own planned property; while browsing around, it became clear that about half of the 24 finished flats on the three floors of Furzedown Court were still unsold and might well be bought "en-bloc" for a significant reduction in the asking price.

Many meetings of the NEC followed where the case for such an ambitious purchase was argued. After hours of discussion and debate, the NEC finally agreed in 1964 to the purchase of the 12 unsold flats in Furzedown Court (one half of the total complex) for the sum of £42,500. The necessary legal conveyance was put in train without delay. The remaining critics of the whole idea took comfort in the view that if Ronnie Greene's scheme failed to work, bricks and mortar could always be sold again.

It was also agreed that it would be appropriate to give a separate name to the Fund's half of the entire block. Maureen Greene, Ronnie's widow takes up the story:

"In 1964, the then-Chairman of the Fund, Don Bates, Chief Fire Officer of Glamorgan Fire Service, and the immediate past chairman, John Fordham, Chief Fire Officer of Kent Fire Brigade, were in favour of renaming our half of the block of flats 'Greene Court' to recognize Ronnie's work for the Fund right back to the war years. But Ronnie was adamant and would have none of it. After some considerable discussion, he finally said 'Call it after Maureen – after all, she has been involved with me in much the Fund has done over the past few years.'

Well, the Chairman and the NEC accepted this view and finalized on a name based upon the way that Ronnie always pronounced my name – Marine – hence Marine Court. For my part, I have always felt it would have been appropriate to call it 'Ronnie's Way'. After all, he did usually get his way in the end!"

Marine Court at Littlehampton was opened as the FSNBF's first convalescent centre in September 1964. Each of the flats had two bedrooms, a reception room, fully fitted kitchen and bathroom and toilet, and was centrally heated. The top floor flats had balconies and a lift served all floors.

However, the first year of Marine Court was far from an easy one. It took many months for the ready availability of Marine Court to be properly utilized and for the 12 flats to be filled on a regular basis. In fact, after Marine Court opened,

Former wartime AFS fireman Fred Munson cuts the ceremonial ribbon during the official opening of Marine Court on 13 May, 1965.

Fred Munson (a former London AFS fireman left permanently disabled during the Blitz when part of a building collapsed on him) and his wife were the only visitors during the autumn months of 1964. However, following a real marketing effort by the Fund within the British fire service that winter, 1965 saw a dramatic improvement in convalescent visitor numbers, with 72 bookings for the year. From then on Marine Court never looked back and with Ronnie and Maureen Greene managing its administration and day-to-day operation, it soon

became evident that it would be prudent for the Fund to consider the purchase of the remaining 12 flats in the block as they became available. This was progressively achieved over the next two years.

In 1974, a further reorganization of local government saw a number of fire brigades being combined. From the post-war total of 144 separate brigades in England, Wales and Scotland, there emerged 63 new county fire brigades including seven large new metropolitan firefighting forces. To coincide with this significant reorganization, changes in the

> *However, the formal opening of Munson House was the last official function that Ronnie attended. He died suddenly at Marine Court, Littlehampton on 2 November, 1978, aged 79…*

Fund's constitution were required. The then chairman, Arthur Bowles, Chief Fire Officer of Lancashire, in conjunction with the Fund's Honorary Solicitor, AJ Pennington, led much of this work.

As the use of Marine Court continued to grow, so did the difficulties experienced when the facilities were used by disabled former members of the fire service. Marine Court itself had no special provisions for these visitors, so there was clearly a need for some sort of dedicated accommodation for the disabled, or for those who required convalescent rest on an unaccompanied basis.

At that time, two separate detached houses situated at No 4 and 6 Maltravers Drive stood alongside the Marine Court complex, and it became evident that these two properties might become available for purchase in the near future. In 1977, Ronnie Greene sought and received approval to acquire the first of these houses, No 6 Maltravers Drive. Once it had been purchased on behalf of the Fund, no time was lost in its refurbishment and conversion.

By the end of the following summer, the house was ready for use. At a special ceremony on 22 September, 1978 the Home Office Assistant Under Secretary of State, Norman Ross, opened the new facility at Littlehampton by renaming No 6 Maltravers Drive "Munson House" in honour of Blitz-disabled former London Auxiliary fireman Fred Munson.

Fred was the Fund's special guest on that day when he proudly cut a ceremonial ribbon of the property now bearing his name. Special donations towards the cost of various items of furnishing for Munson House were received from a number of fire brigades, fire industry manufacturers and non-uniformed supporters of the Benevolent Fund.

Just before the day of the official opening, Ronnie Greene had stood in the garden of Munson House and remarked to his wife Maureen: *"I will not rest until the Fund owns the whole corner of the Fitzalan Road/Maltravers Drive site"*. Four more houses still stood on this site.

However, the formal opening of Munson House was the last official function that Ronnie attended. He died suddenly at Marine Court, Littlehampton on 2 November, 1978, aged 79, still going strong in office as the Fund's Honorary Secretary, a post he had held continuously for over 35 years.

This sad event marked the end of an era for the Fund. Many tributes were paid to Ronnie's work, and his life and times on behalf of the FSNBF. A moving Service of Thanksgiving was held at Southwark Cathedral on 15 December, 1978 where many tributes were addressed to a congregation which included representatives of every British fire brigade. While many members of the fire service had contributed in some way or other to the development and

Ronnie and Maureen Greene pictured outside the entrance to Marine Court, Littlehampton in 1966.

growth of the Fund since the war years, Ronnie Greene was truly its principal architect, guardian and mainspring.

But Maureen, Ronnie's widow, kept up her untiring daily involvement with the Fund which dated back to the 1950s. Along with Ronnie, she had been engaged in the management and administration of Marine Court since its opening in 1964. Upon Ronnie's death, Maureen continued to work vigorously as supervisor and manager of the Littlehampton complex, no doubt mindful that one day there would be a permanent tribute to her husband's lifetime work on behalf of firefighters and their families across the United Kingdom. Fittingly, Maureen's own significant and long term contribution to the Fund was duly marked in the 1980 New Year's Honours List when she was awarded the British Empire Medal.

Maureen continued to work vigorously as supervisor and manager of the Littlehampton complex, no doubt mindful that one day there would be a permanent tribute to her husband's lifetime work on behalf of firefighters and their families across the United Kingdom.

The opening of Marine Court created a steady stream of convalescent visitors, so the Fund needed to acquire a suitable vehicle to collect members and their families from Littlehampton railway station and for general run-about use. The Fund initially purchased an Austin Mini Traveller, but in 1968 firefighters from Mortimer Fire Station, Berkshire and Reading Fire Brigade raised sufficient money to buy a new Hillman Estate for use at Marine Court. Several years later, the much-used Hillman is seen having taken a group of members to visit Guildford Fire Station. It poses for the camera behind a Surrey Fire Brigade water tender.

16 New Homes in Devon, Sussex and Cumbria

DESPITE THE shock waves caused by Ronnie Greene's sudden death, the work of the Fund, both at national and local level, went on. His widow Maureen continued acting as the supervisor and manager of the Marine Court complex. Those who knew Ronnie closely were sure that was what he would have wanted. George Pollock became Honorary Secretary of the FSNBF after Ronnie Greene's death, and over the next few years, he successfully piloted the Fund through a busy and demanding period for all those involved in the management and organization of the charity and its work.

Immediately after his funeral and thanksgiving service, there was a groundswell of opinion that Ronnie Greene's work for the Fund over 35 years should be marked in some visible and permanent manner. This was subsequently carried as a formal motion by the National Council, and the Executive Committee formed a small sub-committee to explore what options were available. At about this time, there was also growing pressure within the National Council that any new property which might be acquired as a second convalescent base should either be in Scotland or the north of England.

Apart from an increasing level of fund-raising income – this topped £1 million for the first time in 1980 – the Fund's investment portfolio had been slowly and prudently broadened since the 1950s. It doubled in value during 1979 to show a book value of just over £3 million. With considerable assets at its disposal, it was not surprising that this was a time of great debate and argument within National Council regarding the best way forward for the Fund.

The Ronnie Greene Memorial Sub-Committee started to search for an ideal property to serve as a second convalescent home. In January 1981, the Fund's Honorary Solicitor, David Ing, found out that a hotel located in a rural situation near Chudleigh, between Exeter and Torquay in Devon, was on the market and might be suitable. The property was being sold under a liquidation order and was likely to be available at an attractive price. Members of the Ronnie Greene Sub-Committee travelled to Devon without delay to inspect the property known as Harcombe House.

They found before them a truly magnificent country property and estate. Built originally in 1912 for the Wills tobacco family, the house faced south with extensive views of Dartmoor and was set in over 300 acres (120ha) of land, 160 acres (65ha) of which was agricultural and 135 acres (55ha) woodland.

There were three lakes stocked for fishing, a stream, a new heated swimming pool, a tennis court and a children's play area. The main house had a dining room capable of seating up to 72 guests,

With considerable assets at its disposal, it was not surprising that this was a time of great debate and argument within National Council regarding the best way forward for the Fund.

4 Maltravers Drive, Littlehampton. This property was acquired by the Fund in 1981.

three large reception rooms, 12 bedrooms (11 with en-suite bathrooms), offices, three staff flats, a stable block which had been converted into a bar, and a large car park. In addition, in the grounds there were 16 fairly new three bedroomed chalets. Most felt that it seemed an ideal proposition.

Immediately after their inspection of Harcombe House on 30 January, 1981, the Ronnie Greene Memorial Sub-Committee formally met in the main house under the chairmanship of Jim Knowlton, the Firemaster of Strathclyde Fire Brigade. The minutes of this meeting record that:

"After a very full and frank discussion about all the aspects of the project and a complete review of the Fund's convalescent rest policy, and the accommodation already owned at Littlehampton, the following proposition was put to the meeting:

That this committee agree to purchase Harcombe House on behalf of the Fund and that an offer of £725,000 be made to the Receiver of the company which own it. This was agreed by 8 votes to 2.

It is known that another prospective purchaser is interested in the property and it was further agreed: That the Honorary Solicitor be authorized to negotiate with the Receiver, if necessary, on the price up to a limit of £750,000. Agreed by 6 votes to 3."

The committee also had another urgent matter to address relating to potential development on the Littlehampton site. In late 1980, the opportunity had arisen for the Fund to acquire "Crofton House" at 4 Maltravers Drive, one of the two remaining houses adjoining Marine Court. The Executive Committee had duly approved the purchase of this property.

At the January 1981 meeting at Harcombe House, Honorary Solicitor David Ing reported that he was now in a position to exchange contracts for the purchase of "Crofton House" if it was the wish of the committee that he should proceed in the light of the decision which had just been taken about Harcombe House. He also confirmed that the owner of "St. Ives", the other remaining property at Littlehampton, had let it be known that he too would be interested in selling to the Fund. If this house were also purchased, it would mean that the Fund would own the entire corner site of Fitzalan Road and Maltravers Drive for future development. The committee unanimously agreed that the exchange of contracts on "Crofton House" should go ahead, and that efforts should be made to purchase

In late 1980, the opportunity had arisen for the Fund to acquire "Crofton House" at 4 Maltravers Drive, one of the two remaining houses adjoining Marine Court.

Formerly 6 Maltravers Drive, Littlehampton, this house was purchased by the Fund in 1977 and refurbished to provide accommodation for members requiring convalescent care on an unaccompanied basis. At its official re-opening on 22 September, 1978 the property was named Munson House in honour of former London AFS fireman Fred Munson, one of the Fund's first disabled members.

Opposite: A view of the frontage of Harcombe House, near Chudleigh in Devon, which was purchased by the Fund in 1981. As well as the house, the estate included a pasture, woodland and heathland setting of 303 acres (123ha), several small staff houses, holiday chalets, and leisure facilities including a swimming pool.

"St. Ives" also. By Easter 1981, the Fund had acquired all three properties to add to its capital assets.

However, once moves were set in motion to open Harcombe House, a serious difficulty arose in linking Ronnie Greene's name with the Devon property and estate. Maureen Greene, who had been kept fully informed of the acquisition of Harcombe House, felt that any memorial to her late husband should be on the Littlehampton site, where Ronnie had done so much pioneering work in the 1960s. The Executive Committee respected her view and when Harcombe House was opened it retained its original name. In the meantime, the search for a suitably appropriate memorial for Ronnie Greene continued.

At the 1981 Annual General Meeting held on 24 April at the Fire Service College, there was some lively criticism of the decision to spend three-quarters of a million pounds on the Devon estate and with such haste. There was even a suggestion that the Fund was becoming a property developer. Chairman Jim Knowlton and several others defended the purchase of Harcombe House pointing out that the sub-committee was empowered to take a rapid decision, otherwise the opportunity would have been lost. The aim was to meet all accommodation requirements at all times. It was pointed out that Fund members needing holiday or convales-

At the 1981 Annual General Meeting held on 24 April at the Fire Service College, there was some lively criticism of the decision to spend three-quarters of a million pounds on the Devon estate and with such haste.

123

Maureen Greene, who had been kept fully informed of the acquisition of Harcombe House, felt that any memorial to her late husband should be on the Littlehampton site, where Ronnie had done so much pioneering work in the 1960s.

One of the chalets at
Harcombe House.

cence could not always be accommodated at Marine Court, especially during the summer months. There were also 200 serving members of the fire service with handicapped children, but Marine Court could only cater for 30 families each year. Jim Knowlton concluded the lengthy discussion by reminding the national representatives that there need be no fears whatsoever about the future because the Fund's constitution prohibits the holding of property or land except for the purposes of the Fund.

Alongside all this democratic debate within the Fund, the steady work to find an appropriate memorial to Ronnie Greene continued apace. Maureen Greene remained of the view that any memorial to her late husband should be on the Littlehampton site. At the 1983 Annual General Meeting the need for the Fund to implement a memorial to Ronnie Greene was stressed by several speakers before the passage of time dulled memories of the origins of the Fund, and Ronnie's important part in it.

After much consultation and examination of a number of schemes, the focus fell upon a possible new building on the site presently occupied by "Crofton House" and "St Ives", the two houses purchased by the Fund in 1981 and sited on the corner adjacent to Marine Court. When National Council met at Bradford for the 1987 AGM, an agreement was finally reached on a scheme for a new £1.14 million purpose-built building to provide sheltered accommodation for members of the Fund.

Thus it was that on 19 April, 1990, HRH Princess Alexandra declared open "The Ronnie Greene Wing" at Littlehampton. This fine three-floor building consisted of eight three-bedroomed and three two-bedroomed self-contained flats, plus two two-bedroomed disabled flats. There were also two single guest rooms together with a caretaker's flat, doctor's consulting room, games room and gymnasium, laundry, lounge/meeting room, and a conservatory. Maureen Greene had been fully involved in the project throughout, personally choosing the décor and fabrics, and was eloquent when she paid tribute to all those involved in the scheme. After the formal opening, Maureen told Princess Alexandra that "Ronnie would be so proud of this special new building".

During the early part of the 1990s demands upon the Fund's property resources continued to grow and a need was identified for a further centre in the north of the United Kingdom. In addition, several research studies had shown that the Fund should try to provide some therapy and remedial treatment for those firefighters who suffered injury which required specialist physiotherapy of some sort. The waiting times for treatment by the National Health Service

126

Thus it was that on 19 April, 1990, HRH Princess Alexandra declared open "The Ronnie Greene Wing" at Littlehampton.

The FSNBF's permanent memorial to the Father of the Fund: the new purpose-built £1.14 million Ronnie Greene Wing in Fitzalan Road, Littlehampton, which was opened by HRH Princess Alexandra on 19 April, 1990.

After the formal opening of the Ronnie Greene Wing at Littlehampton, HRH Princess Alexandra talks to Maureen Greene. No doubt their conversation is about the new building named after Ronnie, a fitting memorial to her husband's 38 years of devoted service to the Fund.

were considerable. Fittingly, in 1993, the Fund's 50th year, the foundation stone was laid at Jubilee House, the first rehabilitation and therapy centre for British firefighters, located in ten acres (4ha) at Eamont Park, Penrith in Cumbria.

Designed and built at a cost of £3.5 million to help members achieve their maximum potential, Jubilee House was designed with great sensitivity for its picturesque Cumbrian setting. Opened formally by HRH Princess Alexandra on 19 April, 1995, the facility includes physiotherapy and hydrotherapy facilities, a gymnasium, and a medical centre. 24-hour convalescent nursing care is also available. The treatment area, known as "The Iain McPhee Wing", was fully equipped entirely thanks to donations given in memory of this 22-year-old firefighter from the West Midlands Fire Service. Iain died on 28 July, 1992 as a result of injuries sustained on duty.

Spacious public rooms enjoy a view of the River Eamont, and two rooms are equipped with specialist bathing facilities for those with disabilities. A leisure pool, a jacuzzi, a sauna and a games area complement the overall amenities of Jubilee House. The site also provides 14 two-bedroomed bungalows and houses for retired firefighters or their widows.

128

On 19 April, 1995, HRH
Princess Alexandra opened
the Fund's first
rehabilitation and therapy
centre for firefighters at
Jubilee House, Eamont Park,
Penrith in Cumbria. This is
the Administration and
Residential Block.

…the facility includes physiotherapy and hydrotherapy facilities, a gymnasium, and a medical centre. 24-hour convalescent nursing care is also available.

The hydrotherapy pool and centre at Jubilee House during an intensive session of therapy for patients with a variety of injuries and medical conditions.

17 FUND-RAISING

Spending more money than is coming in is always a worry for Fund officials.

FUND-RAISING has always been the mainstay of the Fund's income, both during the early wartime days and now in the 21st century. In the year 2000 the Fund's expenditure on its convalescent centre, a therapy centre, sheltered and retirement homes, a range of grants, together with some modest management and administration costs totalled almost £4.2 million. By any standards, this is a huge sum for the supporters of the Fund to have to raise every year to keep the charity solvent. Spending more money than is coming in is always a worry for Fund officials. This was particularly the case during the war years.

In 1944-45, expenditure on death grants and allowances seriously exceeded donations on a number of occasions. In April 1945, cash flow was critical – in the first three months of that year there was a deficit of over £2,000, a large sum in those days. Fortunately, an anonymous well-wisher, not a member of the fire service, paid £1,000 to the FSNBF with the proviso that the Fund should double the sum raised by its own fund-raising efforts during April 1944. This made the target £4,372. Fortunately, the men and women of the National Fire Service rose to the challenge and through local dances, fêtes, jumble sales, raffles, sports competitions and many other initiatives, the sum was raised. During 1945, no less than £45,454 was paid out by the Fund for the relief of hardship alone.

Over the years a quite amazing number and variety of fund-raising schemes, both large and small, have been successfully undertaken to support the Fund's expenditure. Some of the efforts from the early years make for an interesting comparison with fund-raising in more recent times.

• 1947: A collection throughout the NFS sponsored by firewomen and known as the "Shilling Fund" with a nominal target of one shilling donated for every serving British firewoman raised £10,680.
• 1952: Christmas stockings in shops and offices produced donations totalling over £6,000.
• 1952: A cinema appeal film (organized by Ronnie Greene) raised £5,817.
• 1954: A ladies football match in East Lancashire produced £90 and some muddy players! The same area also raised over £30 in a collection of Tide and Daz washing powder packets.
• 1959: A Harvest Festival at Buckley Fire Station, County of Flint Fire Service, North Wales, believed to be a unique event in the British Fire Service, raised £43.13s.9d. County of Flint Fire Service was one of the smaller brigades in the country with only 200 firemen, including retained volunteers, yet through various events over the previous ten years, they raised a collective sum of £5,620 for the Fund.

Local areas of the NFS dreamed up many bright ideas to raise money for the Fund. This poster reveals some of the energy which has gone into the organization of a large Garden Fête in Edinburgh in 1944.

The Fund started a regular Christmas appeal for its orphans at the end of the Second World War. Here is the 1947 example of an appeal stocking which was hung up in thousands of shops and offices throughout the country. Note how the images of the peacetime firemen are faithful to the style of the original Reginald Mills wartime painting reproduced on the cover of this book.

The annual London flag day in March 2001 broke all records. Hundreds of firefighters gave up a whole weekend to collect a massive £94,000 for the Fund.

• 1963: A FSNBF flag day raised a total national sum of £10,290.

More recently fund-raising activities have become much more ambitious in their scope. Here are some examples:

2000: A cycle ride by three West Sussex firefighters from Melbourne to Sydney in Australia, during which they crossed the Snowy and Blue Mountains, produced a cheque for over £1,900.

An epic 1,000-mile (1,600km) 44-day wheelchair journey from John O'Groats to Lands End by former Merseyside firefighter Swasie Turner raised £7,000. Swasie used a standard wheelchair throughout, twice the weight of an athlete's chair.

30 participants flew to Namibia to take part in the Fund's first trek. They crossed dusty plains, climbed high ridges and crossed stunning deep gorges, sleeping under the stars. Each member had to raise £1,800 to participate. The trek netted the Fund a profit of £30,000.

Firefighters from Beckenham Fire Station in London Fire Brigade staged a ladder climb, raising an incredible £14,500. Also in London, a FSNBF Flag Day produced £78,000. Christmas shoppers in Croydon put £10,000 into firefighters' collection buckets.

In the East Midlands, a "Firefighters Challenge" event gave members of the public the chance to try breathing apparatus inside a crawling gallery and maze, thermal-imaging equipment, high pressure hoses and other firefighting kit. This event raised £41,000 with £20,000 coming from Mereway Fire Station, Northampton, and £15,000 from Grantham Fire Station, Lincolnshire.

During the Robin Hood Marathon held in Nottingham, the FSNBF staged an "It's a Knockout" competition as well as a number of other events. In addition 300 firefighters ran in the marathon on behalf of the Fund producing a combined total of £40,000.

The East Midlands area of the Fund also staged a Ladies Driving Challenge Day at Bruntingthorpe Proving Ground in Leicester. 170 women tried their hand at piloting a range of fire engines, tractors, diggers, and HGVs and raised £14,000 in the process.

Towards the end of the year, the Fire Service College in Moreton in Marsh, Gloucestershire hosted a Millennium Appeal in support of the FSNBF and two other fire service charities, the Company of Firefighters and the Firefighters Memorial Charitable Trust. The event included an auction and a Ball; a total of £50,000 resulted.

2001: The annual London flag day in March broke all records. Hundreds of firefighters gave up a whole weekend to collect a massive £94,000 for the Fund. To put this incredible amount in perspective, this sum would enable 80 injured firefighters or their partners to

An early example of a fund-raising event for the Fund. Southampton Fire Brigade firemen from Totton Fire Station get very wet during a water ball competition during the Eling Fair, 1952. The regular firemen are wearing post-war style helmets while the Auxiliary Fire Service crew are using war-issue steel helmets. (Bert Purrington)

benefit from two weeks of intensive therapy at the Fund's Jubilee House Therapy Centre in Cumbria.

Swasie Turner was at it again in April, being the first person to complete the London Marathon in a standard wheelchair. Later in the year Swasie tackled a physically demanding 500-mile (800km) trip from Stroud in Gloucestershire to its twin town, Duderstadt in Germany. This further magnificent effort by Swasie saw more than £2,000 go into the Fund coffers,

and helped to lift the cumulative sums he raised to in excess of £40,000.

The FSNBF international trek was repeated in 2001, this time to China and the Great Wall. Eighty people took part in this hugely successful and ambitious event during June which raised a staggering sum of £104,000.

However, above all things in 2001, it was the terrible events of 11 September in New York that immediately focused the minds of the nation on the fire service. Amid the dust and destruction of

However, above all things in 2001, it was the terrible events of 11 September in New York that immediately focused the minds of the nation on the fire service.

135

Another fine example of solo fund-raising. On 29 May, 1988 Firefighter John Moore of Littlehampton Fire Station, West Sussex Fire Brigade, close to the Fund's Marine Court Headquarters, completed a 40-mile (64km) sponsored run visiting all 14 fire stations in the Brigade's "A" Division. John raised £530 which was used to purchase an exercise machine for the new Ronnie Greene Wing at Marine Court.

Opposite: A highly
successful and unusual
fund-raising day is the
Ladies Driving Challenge
held at Bruntingthorpe
Proving Ground,
Leicestershire. This view
shows the start of the 2001
gathering, the third such
staging of this popular
annual event. Women
participants are about to
try their hand at driving a
wide range of vehicles as
part of the day's fun.

the terrorist attacks on the Twin Towers of the World Trade Center, no fewer than 343 New York firefighters were killed. One fire station alone lost 19 firemen.

Soon after the attack, there was a spontaneous desire expressed throughout British fire brigades to raise funds for the thousands of dependants of the American firefighters. Within days, a major campaign was mounted led by the UK Chief and Assistant Chief Fire Officers' Association (CACFOA) called "The New York Firefighters Appeal". Although the FSNBF was unable to help the New York firefighters directly due to charity regulation constraints, the Fund was able to loan experienced staff to help coordinate various events. These included a musical stage production at the London Palladium.

Right across the United Kingdom, firefighters responded with magnificent fund-raising efforts for the dependants of the New York crews. Many British firefighters were particularly mindful of the way that American firemen had so generously supported the families of the dead and injured of the London Fire Service during the Blitz years when over £30,000 was donated. This was a time when that very special transatlantic support could be, in part, repaid.

Every brigade devoted its efforts to fund-raising. In the first couple of days, West Midlands firefighters took to the streets and collected £20,000. A crew

Many British firefighters were particularly mindful of the way that American firemen had so generously supported the families of the dead and injured of the London Fire Service during the Blitz years…

Swasie Turner, a former Merseyside firefighter and police sergeant, has put a tremendous effort into organizing various fund-raising events for the Fund. His police career came to an abrupt end when he lost a leg after an accident with a motorcyclist who deliberately drove at him. One of Swasie's earlier adventures was a trip to the Falklands, where he undertook a 70-mile (113km) journey over rough terrain from San Carlos to Port Stanley. Here Swasie pauses at Dovercourt Fire Station in Essex during a 500-mile (800km) wheelchair journey from Stroud in Gloucestershire to Duderstadt in Germany.

138

from Alton in Hampshire staged a sponsored car wash outside their fire station to raise the sum of £1,800. Lancashire firefighters raised over £50,000 in a series of street collections, raffles and social evenings. In Surrey, the sum was £20,000, in Somerset over £13,000.

John Pocock, a retired Sub Officer from Thanet, Kent Fire Brigade, organized a 24-hour sponsored swim with both serving and retired members taking part. Cleveland Fire Brigade put on a ladder climb. So the contributions continued to roll in: Tayside Fire Brigade –

> *Over recent years, the Fund has also developed a wide range of merchandise including its mascot Blaze Bear. In various guises, Blaze Bear also gets across the vital message of fire safety.*

over £2,000; The Fire Service College held a bucket collection in the mess and opened a Book of Condolence to be taken personally to New York later in the year; Derbyshire Fire & Rescue Service £41,000; South Yorkshire £65,000; the three fire brigades of Wales £40,000; Gloucestershire £56,000; Wiltshire over £80,000; Manchester in excess of £200,000; Jersey more than £41,000. London, where the Fund was born back in 1940, soon exceeded £200,000. And monies still continued to flow in from fire brigades right up until Christmas 2001, when Hereford and Worcester Fire & Rescue Service donated a staggering £154,144 after staging a disco, quiz nights, car washes and various street collections.

By the end of 2001, British firefighters had raised a massive total in excess of £1.8 million. This sum was passed by CACFOA to the American authorities for distribution to the dependants of the 343 New York firemen killed in the 11 September attack. The terrorist action on that awful day left 1,345 fire service orphans. In a sense, the huge financial assistance given by British firefighters in the weeks after the attack reinvigorated the unique Anglo-American fire service bond that was first established back in the dark days of the London Blitz of 1940. Then US firemen had quickly shown their support for the growing numbers of widows and orphans of the London Fire Service in a tangible man-ner. The aftermath of 11 September allowed British firefighters to close the historical circle.

Further major fund-raising events planned by the FSNBF include a repeat of the Firefighter Challenge Days; over-seas treks to Nepal and (in 2003) to Tanzania and Peru.

Over recent years, the Fund has also developed a wide range of merchandise including its mascot Blaze Bear. In various guises, Blaze Bear also gets across the vital message of fire safety. Other items in the merchandising range include key rings, golf umbrellas, historic fire service prints, statuettes, jewellery and personalized sweatshirts. The FSNBF also provides an affinity credit card for its members through MBNA Europe Bank Ltd. Since 1998, this card alone has raised over £125,000 for the Fund from over 5,500 new accounts.

The range of modern day fund rais-ing initiatives is really quite staggering. A recent guidance leaflet issued by FSNBF listed no fewer than 178 differ-ent ideas ranging from the common-place fire station open days and street collections, to more unusual ideas, such as a sponsored jail break (one of these in 1989 saw three firemen from Humber-side reach Alcatraz, San Francisco!), a bed push, an Easter Bonnet parade, a mile of coins, and even a "Wet The Firefighter" event. Ronnie Greene would surely have been impressed!

18 GOLDEN JUBILEE

140

In celebration of the Fund's Golden Jubilee, Her Majesty The Queen, Patron of the Fire Services National Benevolent Fund, attended a reception held at London's Guildhall on 10 June, 1993. Here the Queen, accompanied by the Fund's Chairman, Firemaster Ian Adam, Central Fire Brigade, Scotland, waves cheerily to the invited guests.

TO COMMEMORATE the Golden Jubilee of the FSNBF, a reception was held at London's Guildhall on 10 June, 1993 in the presence of the Patron of the Fund, Her Majesty The Queen. Some 900 guests were invited, including representatives of every British fire brigade and Fund representatives and many retired firefighters who during their years in uniform had been involved in local fund-raising or other voluntary work for the Fund and its dependants. It was a glittering and memorable occasion when, in addition to the Queen's pres-ence, the tradition and finery of the City of London helped to mark the Fund's first half-century of existence.

At 12 noon, HM The Queen's arrival was heralded by a Change Ringing of the bells of St. Lawrence Jewry by members of the Fire Service Guild of Bellringers. Upon her arrival, the Queen received a bouquet from eight-year-old Hannah Power, whose firefighter father had died the previous year as a result of an acci-dent while on duty.

The Queen was met by the Lord Mayor and City Aldermen, together with the Chairman of the FSNBF, Firemaster Ian Adam of Central Fire Brigade in Scotland. Her Majesty was then invited to meet a profoundly deaf teenage daughter of a serving firefighter, who had been provided with a special hearing aid by the Fund. She was able to tell the Queen how she was training to be a nursery nurse, and her plans for the future. The Queen then met two dis-abled former firefighters in wheelchairs: one had been injured while on duty and the Fund had provided him with a spe-cially adapted car; the other ex-fireman had been disabled by an incurable wast-ing disease and now had the use of an electric wheelchair supplied by the Fund.

A number of other dependants of the FSNBF were presented to Her Majesty. These included a former wartime Control Room Operator who had worked voluntarily for the Fund for

141

30 years; two young sisters and their brother, all under six years of age, whose firefighter father had been badly injured on duty and medically discharged; the nine-year-old daughter of a serving fireman undergoing radiotherapy treatment; and the son of a firefighter killed on duty who was studying for a degree at Cambridge, thanks to a university grant provided by the Fund.

The Queen was then introduced to six special guests who represented a cross section of the many people who had worked for the Fund over the years. This group included 79-year-old former Bristol fireman Geoff Bennett, who had been a founder member of the Bristol area of the Fund back in 1943. Before then, he had served as the first secretary of the Bristol Fire Service Benevolent Fund, one of a number of local organizations which preceded the creation of the National Fund. At the time of the

Guildhall reception in 1993, Geoff was still at working for the Fund in the Avon area, having been involved with fundraising and benevolence continually for over 50 years.

It was appropriate that this Royal Golden Jubilee gathering was held at London's historic Guildhall. For it was in and around this very building, more than 52 years earlier on the night of 29 December, 1940 during the height of the London Blitz, that firemen had fought valiantly to try to restrict the fire damage caused by a particularly concentrated raid. On that fearful night, when a number of firemen were killed in the City of London, incendiary bombs showered down onto the roof of the Guildhall complex. They started many small fires, but although the banqueting hall was badly damaged, other parts of the structure and its priceless fabric and contents were saved.

During the 29 December, 1940 raid, despite the tireless efforts of fire crews, the banqueting hall of the Guildhall and its priceless fabric was badly damaged. Eleven of Wren's fine City churches also suffered severely during the intense raid. (London Fire Brigade)

19 FATAL FIRES

THE ORIGINS of organized firefighting can be traced back to the days of the Roman Empire. Some members of the first *Vigiles* corps in Rome probably lost their lives in the hazardous business of firefighting and rescue. As the first municipal fire brigades were formed in Great Britain during the 19th century, the growing fire risks in an increasingly developing industrial society imposed extra demands upon firemen. Poor housing and workplace conditions meant that many firemen lost their lives or were seriously injured while saving life and protecting property from the ravages of fire.

The hazards persist right up to the present day, and a steady increase in new technology, manufacturing methods and processes, and the advent of man-made hazardous materials, has raised the risk factor facing today's firefighting and rescue crews. Although fire brigades prepare, train and equip their firefighters more intensively than ever before, it can still be a very dangerous occupation as this brief survey of some major incidents from the past 50 years reveals:

21 December, 1952

Eldon Street, London
• British Railways goods warehouse; three firemen killed and 12 seriously injured when part of a high wall fell out into the street; 200 pumps and 500 firemen attended the scene.

23 January, 1958

Smithfield Central Meat Market, London
• Two firemen died when the oxygen of their breathing sets ran out in a smoke-filled basement when they were close to fresh air. The huge underground fire burned for 40 hours through the labryinthine cellars of the market; 1,700 firemen and 390 pumps attended. The subsequent inquiry led to the introduction of the first safety features fitted to breathing apparatus to provide an audible warning to wearers when their oxygen supply was running low.

28 March, 1960

Cheapside Street, Glasgow
• Fourteen firemen of Glasgow Fire Service and five men of Glasgow Salvage Corps were killed when a huge explosion blew apart a bonded whisky warehouse during firefighting operations. Tons of masonry, brickwork and heavy timbers crashed down into the street burying a number of fire engines. Immediately after the fire, the Fund's Executive Committee agreed that the families of the five Glasgow salvagemen should be treated as full dependants of the FSNBF.

15 September, 1965

Esso Refinery, Fawley, Hampshire
• Three firemen were seriously injured during firefighting at a major fire involv-

Although fire brigades prepare, train and equip their firefighters more intensively than ever before, it can still be a very dangerous occupation...

A work by fireman artist Reginald Mills entitled "Night Rescue". It depicts the dramatic true-life 1945 rescue by Fireman Frederick Davies of two young children trapped in a burning bedroom above a shop in Harlesden High Street, Middlesex. Davies crawled off the escape ladder into the smoke-filled room and located both children, and got them to the window. As he passed them to another fireman on the ladder, the entire room behind him burst into flames. Hardly had the second child been taken from his hands than he collapsed back into the inferno. Davies was posthumously awarded the George Cross. He left a wife and two children, aged ten months and six years.

143

144

A London fireman
overcome by heat and
smoke is carried to a
waiting ambulance during
firefighting operations at a
large fire in an East London
warehouse, 11 May, 1954.
(London Fire Brigade)

Fourteen firemen of Glasgow Fire Service and five men of Glasgow Salvage Corps were killed when a huge explosion blew apart a bonded whisky warehouse during firefighting operations.

Flames lick high into the night sky following a huge explosion in a bonded whisky warehouse which blew out part of the building and killed 14 Glasgow firemen and five men of the Glasgow Salvage Corps. This tragedy is still the worst disaster in the peacetime history of the modern fire service. The location is Cheapside Street, Glasgow, 28 March, 1960. (*Scottish Daily Express*)

146

A picture taken on 29
March, 1960, the morning
after the Cheapside Street
blaze. Hundreds of tons of
bricks and timber have
crashed into the street
completely crushing the
Glasgow Fire Service
turntable ladder in the
foreground. (Strathclyde
Fire Brigade)

ing fuel storage tanks. It was attended by 37 pumps and 200 firemen.

16 February, 1966
RAF Neatishead, Norfolk
• Two retained firemen lost their lives while wearing breathing apparatus in a deep-seated underground fire at this military establishment.

22 October, 1967
Kellogg's, Stretford, Lancashire
• Nine firemen seriously injured during a major fire which involved 47 pumps from 11 different fire brigades in an extensive firefighting operation.

17 July, 1969
Dudgeons Wharf, Millwall, London
• Five firemen killed in an explosion in a derelict fuel tank farm during the demolition of disused oil tanks.

25 August, 1972
Kilbirnie Street, Glasgow
• Seven firemen killed during a serious fire in a clothing warehouse. Following a flashover, one fireman was reported missing inside the building. Several rescue teams immediately entered the burning premises to search for their missing colleague, only themselves to become fatal casualties.

18 November, 1972
Maryhill Road, Glasgow
• One fireman killed during a basement fire beneath shops, with offices and tenements above. He had taken off his breathing set to give it to a resident who had been overcome by smoke. Five firemen were also injured.

5 October, 1973
Off the coast of Plymouth, Devon

Tons of masonry, brickwork and heavy timbers fell out into the street burying a number of fire engines.

The funeral cortège of the 19 men killed in the Cheapside Street fire sombrely passes Central Fire Station in Ingram Street where many of the firemen had been stationed. Thousands of Glaswegians lined the route in silent tribute to their firemen, bringing much of the centre of the city to a standstill. (Strathclyde Fire Brigade)

One fireman killed and three others badly burned when buried during a building collapse at a major hotel fire...

148

The sudden collapse of the building during the major fire at the Worsley Hotel in central London on 13 December, 1974 buried four firefighters. It took three hours to get them all out. Here the second trapped fireman to be released, Station Officer Colin Searle of Westminster Fire Station, is carried carefully away to an ambulance. His eyes tell some of the story of this dramatic rescue. Tragically, one of the buried crew lost his life. (London Fire Brigade)

Opposite: A newspaper cutting reporting a serious fire in a builders' merchants in Reading which claimed the lives of two firefighters on 15 September, 1977. (*Reading Mercury*)

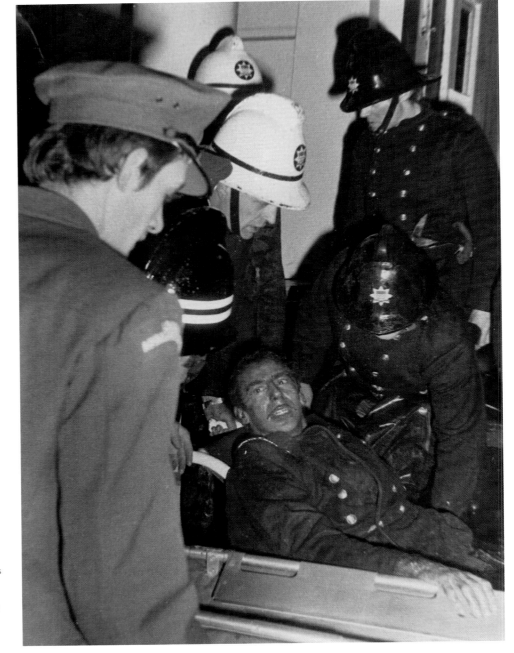

Mercury, Thursday, September 22nd, 1977

Berks blaze battle that cost two men's lives

There was a new drama on Thursday night when a wall collapsed during the search for the second victim. A dozen firemen just managed to scramble clear.

THE blaze which claimed the lives of two Berkshire firemen and completely destroyed a builders' merchants warehouse erupted shortly after 11 a.m. on Thursday last week.

Secretaries and typists working in offices on the second floor of the building in Elgar Road, Reading, had noticed smoke coming from a paint and wallpaper storeroom.

But it was not until the firm's security and safety officer went to investigate that the full horror of the blaze began to unfold.

The two firemen who died were among the first crews to arrive at the scene, minutes after the alarm was raised.

Family men killed as fire wrecks warehouse complex in the heart of Reading...

'MERCURY' REPORT BY PHIL COOPE. PICTURES BY BOB BODMAN AND NEIL LOFTHOUSE

They were Neil Mark Goldsmith, of Wigmore Road, Tadley, and David Barton, of The Mayfair, Tilehurst. Both men were married with children.

Fireman Goldsmith, who was 31, leaves a daughter of five and a son aged four. He joined the Berkshire Fire Brigade in 1974 and served at Slough before being moved to the Wokingham Road station in Reading in February 1977. He had previously been a part-time fireman at Tadley.

Fireman Barton, 44, was married with a son aged 18 and a daughter of 14. He had served at the Caversham Road, Reading, fire station since joining the Berkshire brigade from the London Fire Service in 1969.

At the height of the blaze over 100 firemen from Berkshire and neighbouring counties battled to stop the flames spreading to other buildings.

Off-duty firemen were telephoning their volunteer...

...tearing to help while mobile canteens and emergency first-aid posts were set up at the scene.

The fire which wiped out Clarks' Builders Merchants and sent an estimated £1 million started in a small wallpaper store. The flames spread quickly to an adjoining store containing thousands of gallons of paint.

The firm's safety and security officer, ex-police sergeant Bill Amor, raised the alarm after a receptionist told him she had seen smoke seeping from the paint store.

Mr. Amor then ran down to the paint store and was met...

...with a wall of flame. "I nudged open the door but the room was already full of smoke and flames were licking along the roof."

The 150 members of staff and dozens of customers were evacuated from the building within three minutes. Neighbouring offices and factories were also evacuated in case the flames spread to other buildings.

The two firemen who died were among the crew of two appliances which raced to the scene from the Caversham Road station.

One of the victims was sent on to the roof to try to contain the flames to stop them spreading to the front of the building.

But the highly inflammable materials stored below — paint, turpentine, wallpaper and plas...

...tic — fuelled the flames into an inferno.

The top floor collapsed and the fireman was sent plunging into the heart of the blaze in the basement.

His colleague had gone into the building wearing breathing apparatus to ensure that everybody had managed to get clear, when the floors above him collapsed.

When news broke that the men were missing the Chief Fire Officer for Berkshire, Mr. Dick Barton, had to restrain his men from dashing into the blazing building in a bid to pull them out.

Shortly after 1 p.m., more than two hours after the blaze started, any hopes of saving the building were ended when a turpentine store exploded.

Mr. Barton refused to risk the lives of more of his men...

...until the building was safe for them to go in and search for their colleagues.

They had been missing for nearly four hours when demolition experts were called in to help firemen pull down the crumbling front of the building.

But at 4.45, while parts of the gutted warehouse were still smouldering, firemen wearing breathing apparatus climbed down into the basement.

While they were manhandling the debris one masonry was falling around them and paint tins were exploding in the heat.

It was not until the bodies had been located that Mr. Barton finally gave up hope for his men. The first body was brought out just after five...

...o'clock while dozens of firemen stood with heads bowed and tears in their eyes.

Minutes later, a demolition worker shouted a warning and a dozen men scrambled to safety as a large section of the building suddenly collapsed.

The second body was located at 6.20 p.m. but it was some time before it could be brought out.

Throughout the day, scores of police were at the scene trying to keep hundreds of sightseers away and to keep the roads clear for emergency vehicles.

Firemen were still damping down the gutted shell of the building on Friday morning when police and fire experts arrived to begin the task of discovering the cause of the blaze.

A thick pall of smoke rises from the devastated building.

Over 100 firemen called in to tackle inferno

From the rear of the premises, smoke and flames engulf walls and roof.

For some time the hoses could make little impact on the flames raging within the building.

The agonised expression on his face tells of this exhausted fireman's ordeal.

Fighting the fire through the shattered front windows.

Smoke pours from inside a burning Woolworth's store in Manchester on 8 May, 1979 as a hydraulic platform crew direct a powerful jet into the building to bring the fire under control. Ten shoppers died in the fire which led to a new fire safety standard being applied to upholstered furniture.

• Ten firemen injured in an explosion during operations while fighting a fire on board the MV *Barrad Crest*.

13 December, 1974
Worsley Hotel, London
• One fireman killed and three others badly burned when buried during a building collapse at a major hotel fire after many successful rescues had been carried out.

27 March, 1977
Dover, Kent
• One fireman killed during a fire at a block of flats.

15 September, 1977
Reading, Royal Berkshire
• Two firefighters killed in a building collapse during firefighting in a builders' merchant. A crew had been working in

breathing sets on the ground floor when it suddenly collapsed into the basement. One fireman was pulled out alive but, within a minute or so, the first floor and roof fell in taking another fireman with it. Despite strenuous and determined rescue efforts, the two buried firemen were dead when they were extricated. Several local funds were soon started in Reading, quickly raising over £4,000 in excess of the two widow's grants of £2,000 each paid by the FSNBF. The total proceeds of the local funds finally topped £10,000 and, in accordance with the wishes of those concerned, this sum was donated to the FSNBF.

21 May, 1981
Fort Augustus, Inverness
• One volunteer fireman killed and another seriously injured during a fire at a guest house.

One fire officer killed during rescue attempts after fire engulfed an escalator and swept into the booking hall... He was posthumously awarded the George Medal.

27 November, 1987: the funeral of a hero. Station Officer Colin Townsley of Soho Fire Station died while attempting to rescue passengers trapped underground during a major fire in King's Cross Underground Station. Here his coffin is borne on a flower-decked turntable ladder to a full funeral service at which every British fire brigade was represented. Colin Townsley was posthumously awarded the George Medal. (London Fire Brigade)

151

18 November, 1987
King's Cross Underground Station, London
• One fire officer killed during rescue attempts after fire engulfed an escalator and swept into the booking hall, trapping many commuters. He was posthumously awarded the George Medal. Thirty passengers died in this tragedy.

5 November, 1990
Penzance, Cornwall
• A firefighter died while undergoing routine training using a 100-foot (30m) turntable ladder.

27 July, 1992
Charlecote Tower, Dorking Grove, Birmingham
• During firefighting operations, two firemen were caught in a flashover during a serious fire in a high-rise block of flats. Another firefighter entered the burning flat and carried one of the badly burnt firemen to safety, and he was then joined by another colleague in the rescue of the remaining casualty. Sadly, this fireman subsequently died from his injuries. Both rescuers were honoured for their bravery, one with the George Medal, the other with the Queen's Gallantry Medal.

...such fatal fires always bring the work of the FSNBF into sharp focus, for the Fund and its voluntary officials spring into action soon after these tragic instances occur.

Opposite: Willing hands come to the aid of an injured Tyne and Wear firefighter on 9 October, 1990. (*Newcastle Chronicle & Journal*)

1 February, 1996

Blaina, South Wales

• Two retained firefighters died when they entered a burning terraced house for the second time and were caught in a flashover. They had readily gone back inside when informed that a child was still trapped inside the property. Both firefighters were awarded posthumous gallantry awards.

4 February, 1996

Speedwell, Bristol

• A female firefighter was killed, the first such peacetime death, when she was caught by a flashover inside a supermarket while searching in breathing apparatus for shoppers who were believed to be missing amid the thick smoke. Her male team member was awarded a George Medal for his gallant attempt to rescue his female colleague. She was posthumously awarded the Queen's Gallantry Medal. An arsonist was subsequently convicted and sentenced to seven and a half years imprisonment.

These various incidents involving firefighter fatalities and serious injuries are just some of those which have occurred in the years since the FSNBF was formed. They have been chosen simply to represent the wide range of fires and other emergencies which the fire service attends every day and night of the year. Sadly, there have been other fire service fatalities and serious injuries not mentioned above.

Collectively, such fatal fires always bring the work of the FSNBF into immediate sharp focus, for the Fund and its voluntary officials spring into action soon after these tragic instances occur.

It should also be noted that at some of the serious fires described above, members of the public also sadly lost their lives, in most cases despite the gallant rescue efforts of firefighters.

Since the Second World War, fire brigades have been increasingly called to "non-fire" emergencies, such as road and rail crashes, leakages of hazardous chemicals, machinery and underground-working accidents, and many types of animal rescues. These emergency calls are termed "special services", and in carrying them out firefighters have occasionally lost their lives.

One of the first recorded instances of a special service firefighter fatality occurred in Sheffield in 1950 when a fireman fell out of a tree during an attempt to retrieve a cat high up in its branches. Even freak weather conditions produce hazardous circumstances – during the memorable hurricane of October 1987, two members of Dorset Fire Brigade were killed whilst responding to the effects of the wild weather. Needless to say, the Fund is quick to respond to the tragic consequences of special service incidents.

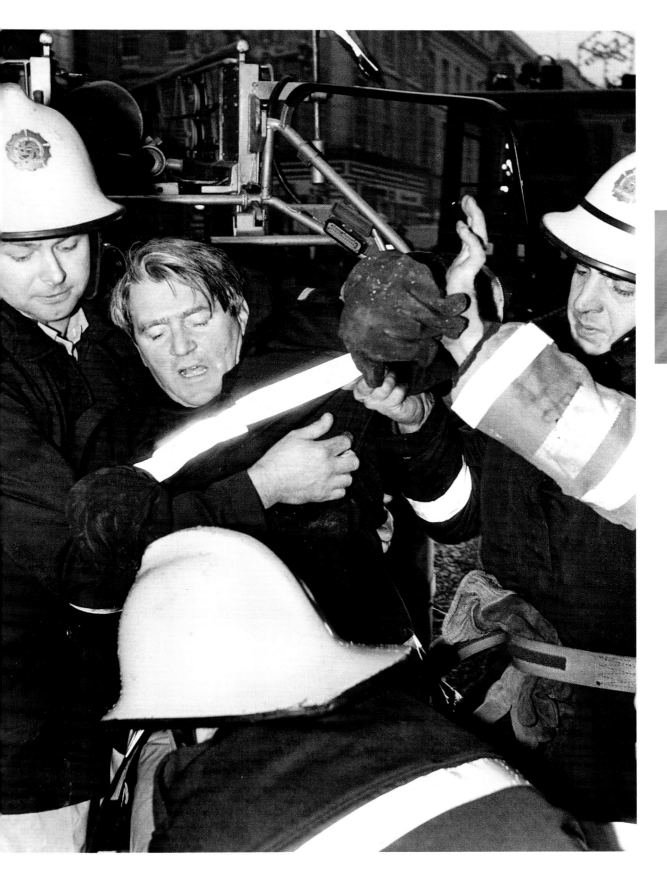

20 THE FUND AT WORK

Opposite: Mrs Sandra Bermingham's husband was one of seven firemen killed during a serious fire in a warehouse in Kilbirnie Street, Glasgow on 25 August, 1972. Since that date, the Fund has provided regular educational grant support for both of her children, Alison and Iain, all the way through to their university degree courses. Sandra's eldest child, Alison, who was five when her father was killed, is shown on graduation day at Glasgow University when she attained her degree in microbiology. She later achieved a doctorate. Since then she has been working in the United States.

IN THE optimistic spring of 1945 with the war in Europe clearly moving towards an Allied victory, the officers of the FSNBF started to consider how the Fund should prepare for and adapt to meet the different benevolent needs of firefighters in time of peace.

The National Executive Committee approved a special leaflet distributed to every member of the NFS which briefly set out the way ahead, emphasizing that although the Fund was a product of the war years, it would continue to support members, mostly AFS recruits, who would shortly be leaving the fire service, as well as maintaining financial help to the widows of those firefighters who had fallen in action and the 1,343 orphans of the Fund.

When Ronnie Greene drafted the text for this leaflet, he used a few words which succinctly sum up what the Fund had achieved up to 1945 and what its aspirations were for the future:

"The Fund has always tried to help, not only by monetary assistance, but also by information, advice, guidance, and real practical sympathy; in other words – *the alleviation of distress*."

Despite all that has been written about the work of the FSNBF since the end of the Second World War, this sentence still best sums up what the Fund is all about. However, some brief extracts from the Fund's 1945 records show that many dependants' cases were far from straightforward.

Former Fireman W.

This smiling young officer often asserts he owes his life to the Benevolent Fund. He was one of many victims of the London Blitz – his back was broken when the burning building in which he was working crashed to the ground. Encased in plaster in hospital, paralysed from the waist down, and very seriously ill, it was doubtful if he would live. But the Fund continued with visits, little luxuries, kind messages and enquiries from old comrades and slowly helped to re-awaken his will to live. Two long years were to follow before he was able to sit up. The Fund was able to provide a wheel chair and in 1946, when he was well enough, he was one of the first members to receive a motorized version.

Former Fireman F.

Married with young baby. Discharged from the service with facial injuries caused by bomb blast. Still attending hospital three days a week with a corneal ulcer, likely to go blind. Earns 25 shillings per week on part-time work. Grants

The Fund has always tried to help, not only by monetary assistance, but also by information, advice, guidance, and real practical sympathy…

from Fund total £151 so far, also clothing supplied for wife and child.

Former Firewomen G.

Middle-aged woman discharged from the service with chronic bronchitis and asthma. Total income 9 shillings per week. Received £160 from the fund to date.

Former Fireman AR.

Married, wife unable to work. Left leg amputated following gangrene. Injury not attributable to service. Income 10/6d per week from National Health Insurance. Over £210 granted by Fund; assistance being given in providing artificial limb and motorized wheelchair.

Former Fireman C.

Married, seven children, eighth expected. Fund helped to get one child into children's convalescent home following pneumonia and measles. Other children undernourished and ill-clad. In arrears with rent. Grants of £18 from Fund towards clothing for all the family. Fund successfully pressed local authority to implement urgent house improvements.

The modern-day work of the Fund is no less wide-ranging as is well illustrated by a few accounts of more recent

assistance provided to former members and their families.

Mrs Sandra Bermingham

Sandra's husband was a serving fireman in Glasgow Fire Service when he was one of seven men who died during firefighting operations at a serious fire in a clothing warehouse in Kilbirnie Street, Glasgow, in August 1972.

156

Sandra was left a widow with a daughter, Alison aged five. Sandra was also three months pregnant with her second child, Iain, who was born in January 1973.

Apart from the full financial and general support provided by the Fund for a widow, both Alison and Iain received orphan's grants and educational allowances to assist them through their school years and then on to further education. Both Sandra's children gained degrees at Glasgow University; Alison in microbiology and Iain in media studies. Alison went on to achieve a doctorate at St. Andrew's University and since then has worked as a Doctor of Microbiology at the American National Institute for Health in Washington, D.C. During the children's earlier years, Sandra was also able to take several recuperative holidays at Marine Court, Littlehampton. Now, over 30 years since the Kilbirnie Street tragedy, Sandra is still full of praise for the support of the Fund and its representatives in the Strathclyde Fire Brigade, and of the practical help and assistance she has received over the years.

Mrs Marie Tilley

Marie's husband, John, served in the London Fire Service for 25 years but sadly died in 1994. Marie started to suffer from rheumatoid arthritis and a few heart problems and had

The Fund was able to provide a new racing green wheelchair to improve Marie's mobility.

Joe Roberts joined the Auxiliary Fire Service in London during the early days of the Blitz when he was only 16. He served as a motorcycle despatch rider through all the action of the later war years. In November 2001 it was believed that Joe was probably the last surviving fire service DR. As a contribution to the FSNBF, Joe undertook (by car!) a nationwide tour of various fire stations (including the Fund's three centres) dressed in his original wartime uniform. Here Joe pauses outside No 10 Downing Street to deliver a message of goodwill to the Prime Minister about the work of the Fund. Sadly Joe died during 2002.

difficulties in getting out and about. The Fund was able to provide a new racing green wheelchair to improve Marie's mobility.

Firefighter Stuart Damen, Hampshire Fire & Rescue Service

Stuart serves at Southsea Fire Station, and for many years had been an active worker for the FSNBF. When Loren, his daughter aged 6, was diagnosed as suffering from San Filippo disease, a rare genetic disorder, he obviously pursued everything possible to alleviate her condition. Stuart also found time to raise some funds for the San Filippo Society, a research-based fund dedicated to finding a cure for the disease.

The FSNBF were able to provide a grant to Stuart to help adapt the family home to properly care and accommodate Loren. The family were also placed on a "Young Special Needs Register" so that ongoing assistance can be provided

...the Fund has been able to assist Ian to keep him mobile, paying for the deposit and hand controls to his Motability car.

One of the Fund's services that members particularly value is the provision of mobility aids. During 2002, Francis Edwards, an 89-year-old former London fireman now living in retirement at Bembridge on the Isle of Wight, was provided with a new stairlift. It was supplied and fitted by the Fund. Here he tries out the stairlift watched by the former IOW Brigade Fund Secretary, Tony Kennedy.

Extract from a letter from
Mrs Enid Harvey, Rugeley,
Staffordshire.

159

"...I am registered partially sighted and find it a little difficult to write. Many thanks to everyone for the very generous grant paid to me, I appreciate it very much. The FSNBF have been very good to me since my husband died. The Benevolent Fund does such a great job and the firefighters work so hard to raise the money."

on an annual basis. The Damens are also able to avail themselves of beneficial rest at one of the Fund's centres.

Former Firefighter Ian Glasham, Bedfordshire Fire Service

Ian joined Bedfordshire Fire Service in 1972 as a retained firefighter and it was not long before he was helping to raise funds for the FSNBF at Open Days and the like. Little did he know that he would be shortly needing the help of the Fund himself for, in 1980, Ian was involved in a motorcycle accident which left him paraplegic – totally wheelchair bound.

Since then the Fund has been able to assist Ian to keep him mobile, paying for the deposit and hand controls to his Motability car. Ian and his parents have also had a regular break at one of the Fund's convalescent centres.

To recognize Ian's earlier work for the Fund, in the summer of 2000 he was invited to join the Bedfordshire Fund Committee where he volunteered to become a representative of the Fund's "Less Able" members, ultimately taking on this role at a national level. Ian has already got a number of Bedfordshire firefighters to sign up

Opposite: In 2001 the Fund was able to provide a vehicle steplift for Isobel Lea, the daughter of a Hampshire firefighter. Isobel's father, Philip, says the lift has made a dramatic difference to their lives and has given Isobel a new level of mobility and independence. She is immensely proud of the device. Here, Isobel is pictured with her father alongside a water tender from Droxford Fire Station.

to the Gift Aid scheme and is clearly inspiring many others in his area to continue to support the work of the Fund.

Former Firefighter Dick Foggie, London Fire Brigade

Dick is a former member who is now confined to a wheelchair. In late 2001 he attended Jubilee House in Cumbria for the first time. After his two-week course at Jubilee House, Dick wrote to thank all concerned for the help he had received:

"Having spent much of the last five years in various medical establishments, I wasn't too keen on letting the white coat brigade get hold of me. Good sense prevailed and my experience was both incredible and enjoyable.

The comfort and disabled facilities of my room would put a private hospital to shame. Without exception, the staff, medical, clerical and domestic were enthusiastic, friendly and very professional."

Firefighter Jan Eley, West Midlands Fire Service

Jan, a firefighter for 27 years, injured his back after falling from a roof during firefighting operations at a fire at Foresthill in Coventry. He

damaged his spinal cord, dislocated a vertebra and broke two other bones in his back. There was a fear that he would never walk again but after weeks of physiotherapy at Jubilee House, Jan was back on his feet.

Leading Firefighter Matt Smith, Oxfordshire Fire Service

During an off-duty inter-brigade football match in South Wales in the late 1990s, Matt went down heavily in a goalmouth scramble with several other players falling on top of him, injuring his back. He was off sick for a week but despite some discomfort returned to full firefighting duty and took part in a breathing apparatus drill. As he wriggled through a window, he suffered intense back pain and was forced to take sick leave again.

Matt remained in constant pain and an NHS consultant advised therapy treatment before considering the option of surgery to correct two diagnosed prolapsed discs. The local Fund representative was quickly able to get Matt booked in for a two-week physiotherapy course at Jubilee House, Penrith, where he was placed in one of three treatment groups according to a patient's particular needs. Matt's group spent a considerable time in

The comfort and disabled facilities of my room would put a private hospital to shame. Without exception, the staff, medical, clerical and domestic were enthusiastic, friendly and very professional.

Extract from a letter from
Mrs Rita Hicks, Milton-
under-Wychwood,
Oxfordshire.

"Please accept my grateful thanks for the generous grant made to me. It helps so much financially and I appreciate all the fund-raising achieved by the firefighters and staff over the years. My late husband (ex-London Fire Brigade) and now my eldest son (also LFB) have always undertaken many events for the FSNBF (including acting as Blaze Bear and Father Christmas) and I am very aware of the great efforts and hard work involved."

Extract from a letter from
Mr G. Horn, Brandon.

" I would like to thank you for your help. I received the electric scooter on Friday and already I've been able to go out around the town and talk to people that I have not seen for a long time. It has already changed my way of life. I should like to thank the Benevolent Fund for paying for the scooter and giving me a new outlook on life after not being very mobile."

164

Opposite: Some of Hereford & Worcester's firefighters during their fund-raising effort for the New York Fire Department's widows and orphans of the 11 September Twin Towers attack in 2001. The brigade raised over £154,000 towards a collective British Fire Service contribution which totalled in excess of £1.8 million.

hydrotherapy exercises in the pool. A personally tailored exercise programme was also provided for Matt to follow once he returned home.

At the end of two weeks, he was well enough to go back to Rewley Road Fire Station, Oxford on day duty non-operational work, such as fire safety inspections and school visits, but was still finding his back injury painful. Several months of day duty passed by, and the likelihood of medical retirement started to loom in Matt's mind. Fortunately, he was determined to return to full firefighting duties and was able to secure another two-week intensive therapy course at Jubilee House. At the end of this, he was able to return to full duty and is full of praise for the skill and special care he received from the medical team at Penrith. "Without their careful work, I am sure I would not have got back to front-line duty when I did and may have had to leave the service altogether".

More recently, Matt's wife Jane, coincidentally also suffered a disc injury during childbirth. She was also able to attend an intensive therapy course at Jubilee House which provided a complete cure.

Without their careful work, I am sure I would not have got back to front-line duty when I did and may have had to leave the service altogether.

21 THE NEW CENTURY

Opposite: In recent years some of the cast of the "London's Burning" television programme have become actively involved in a concerted campaign to promote the Fund's Covenant scheme and subsequently its Gift Aid programmes. Here the television firefighters pose in front of their pumps outside London's "Blackwall" Fire Station.

WITH THE coming of the new millennium, the FSNBF was equipping itself to take on the challenges of fund-raising in the 21st century.

The Gift Aid programme – previously known as the Covenant scheme – went from strength to strength during 2000 with a spectacular total of 21,545 persons signing up to give regularly to the Fund. By the end of that year, this hugely successful scheme had produced an annual income of £815,315. Over £230,000 of this sum was from tax reclaims. The cast of the very successful television series "London's Burning" readily gave their time to promote both the earlier Covenant scheme and Gift Aid package.

The sum raised benefited greatly during the year thanks to a number of changes in the Gift Aid scheme implemented by the government. This means that if a donor is a taxpayer or pays capital gains tax, charities such as the Fund are now able to reclaim the tax on all donations, even from a one-off contribution on a sponsorship form. This change enabled the Fund to collect extra cash that would previously have been lost to the Exchequer.

The Gift Aid programme was developed and coordinated by an Administrator at Marine Court, supported by individual representatives in fire brigades who promote this particular scheme. One of these was Station Officer John

The cast of the very successful television series "London's Burning" readily gave their time to promote both the earlier Covenant scheme and Gift Aid package.

Another major development of the new century was the launch of the FSNBF website at www.fsnbf.org.uk

Scott, attached to Finchley Fire Station in London Fire Brigade. He noted that the London brigade was only donating £20,000 per year through the scheme; John went to work and soon had every firefighter on all four watches (shifts) at Finchley signed up. He then started on the other 112 fire station of the London Fire Brigade. By the end of 2000, 1,717 new Gift Aid declarations from personnel in the London Fire Brig-ade had helped to lift the annual contribution to £217,185 with an additional £61,257 coming from reclaimed tax.

John Scott retired in December 2000 after 34 years service, but that did not stop him. He helped Fund colleagues in the Durham and Darlington brigade to promote the Gift Aid scheme, securing 225 extra declarations (extra annual income £12,156); then went on to Strathclyde (239 extra covenants – £15,146) and is currently at work supporting the scheme in the Greater Manchester brigade.

During 2000, Gift Aid pledges rose by 21 per cent, a very important and relatively new form of income for the Fund. John Scott continues to play a significant part in this effort, and his enthusiasm and energy is typical of the many firefighters who continue to have an active involvement with the Fund well after their retirement date.

Another major development of the new century was the launch of the

FSNBF website at www.fsnbf.org.uk. A one-stop information point containing over 20 pages, the site is full of news and essential facts about the Fund and its work. Information on the website includes details of fund-raising activity, donations, the Gift Aid scheme, a calendar of events, news, training and welfare issues, together with the full range of Fund merchandise.

During the early part of 2000, a pilot welfare advice scheme was extended nationally with a free Helpline set up at Marine Court Headquarters to advise on a range of issues likely to be of concern to members, issues such as convalescence, welfare rights and an approved list of suppliers of mobility equipment. Over 12,000 Welfare Helpline cards with the dedicated telephone number were distributed through fire brigades and firefighter pensioner groups.

To assist in the speedy exchange of information, and to provide a rapid response to an urgent welfare request, an extensive e-mail national network was commissioned in 2000 linking Marine Court Headquarters with Harcombe House, Jubilee House, and all Fund representatives throughout the United Kingdom. This has proved to be an immensely valuable link to all beneficiaries, dedicated volunteers and fund-raisers.

An even more recent fund-raising scheme has seen the introduction of a FSNBF Lottery with a guaranteed

Blaze Bear was introduced in 1998 as the national mascot of the Fund. Originally created as a "thank you" to firefighters after a house fire from which over 500 priceless antique bears were dramatically rescued, Blaze Bear has helped the Fund to raise awareness of fire safety issues. He also brings in vital income through a wide range of Blaze Bear merchandise. These include Trauma Teds, designed to provide comfort to traumatized children who have been involved in a fire. Here six-year-old Nicola Fuller tests out 50 Trauma Teds donated to West Sussex Fire Brigade by Amex.

£25,000 jackpot each month. This scheme began in the autumn of 2002 and is likely to provide another source of regular income for the Fund.

The many people who make the FSNBF work at both national and local level – uniformed members of fire brigades across Great Britain, officials and civilian staff – all continue to display tremendous commitment and enthusiasm for their work.

Many have served the Fund in different ways for decades. Honorary Treasurer David Ing was awarded the MBE in the 2001 New Year's Honours List for his long and tireless work for the Fund over 26 years. He retired later in that year, only the fourth person to hold that important post in the Fund's history. In 2001, National Council decided to recognize particularly long and outstanding service to the Fund by a

170

Twenty-first century firefighting. A West Yorkshire crew clad in the latest style of personal protection get to grips with the hot stuff during a large fire in a yard full of timber pallets at Horbury, Wakefield in July 2001. (Brian Saville, West Yorkshire Fire Service)

171

National Merit Award. The first of these was presented to Elsie Fernihough for her work for the Fund over a period of 50 years. Elsie had served in the NFS during the Liverpool Blitz, represented Merseyside on the Fund's National Council for many years, and is still active in fund-raising events.

These are but two of a small army who today make the FSNBF work. It is now more than 60 years since the Fund came into existence at beginning of the London Blitz. Throughout this period of time it has been a constant challenge to keep the Fund's income abreast of expenditure coupled with the constant understated desire to improve benevolence grants and general assistance to those in need.

Today the FSNBF and all those connected with its work can be rightly proud of the Fund's impressive achievements. These range from its convalescent centres, sheltered accommodation, and therapy centre right down to structured help for disabled children, various mobility packages and, at the other end of the scale, modest yet important offerings such as Christmas hampers given to fire service pensioners and widows.

The growth of the National Fund from such modest beginnings in 1943 is a direct tribute to all those many supporters who over the past 60 years have readily contributed plenty of time, effort and enthusiasm to a most noble cause.

Today the FSNBF and all those connected with its work can be rightly proud of the Fund's impressive achievements.

22 EPILOGUE

Opposite: Another fire service casualty of the London Blitz. In the harsh first light of dawn on 17 September, 1940, a London Fire Service fireman lies dead in a Southwark street after a night of intense raiding. This took place during the period of 57 nights of continual Blitz bombing. The poster on the right proclaims "Fall in the Fire Bomb Fighters" – a quote attributed to the Home Secretary, Herbert Morrison MP.

WHEN I was invited to write *Out of the Flames* and capture in words and pictures the events of the past 60 years of the FSNBF, I realized that this might be the most challenging writing commission that I had yet taken on. And so it has proved…

Fortunately, like all who have served in the British fire service, it helped that I have first-hand understanding and experience of the way the Fund operates at local level, particularly when a major tragedy strikes.

On the cold and windy night of Friday 13 December, 1974, while a young Station Commander at Paddington Fire Station in the London Fire Brigade, my crews responded to multiple "999" fire calls calling them to a six-floor hotel on our patch in the Maida Vale district. An arsonist had lit several fires on different floors. As we arrived, there were about 36 residents trapped on high ledges screaming for help as fire and smoke threatened to sweep up and engulf them.

The fire, at the Worsley Hotel, quickly became a 30-pump affair, London's biggest fire that year. All 36 residents were rescued inside the first few minutes of the arrival of the London Fire Brigade in a series of highly dramatic and risky rescues using wheeled escape and hook ladders. Fortunately nobody jumped before firemen got up to them, and everyone was carefully coaxed down to safety.

After about an hour of intense physical firefighting, the blaze was just beginning to come under some semblance of control, with crews in breathing apparatus probing ever deeper into smoke-filled corridors and rooms searching for a number of residents who were still unaccounted for.

Then suddenly the fire fought back. Part of the roof at one end of the long frontage of the hotel collapsed and fell into the fifth floor, which in turn collapsed into the fourth and so on. The accumulated weight of burning timber, hot brickwork and masonry crashed into a second floor bedroom completely burying a four-man firefighting crew who unfortunately were working there.

Three members of this crew were from my command; two of these were fresh out of Training School and in their probationary period, while the third was an experienced veteran of many serious fires in London's West End. The final trapped firefighter was a fellow Station Commander and a good friend of mine, based at Westminster Fire Station. The rescue of the four buried men took three hours. One by one they were carefully dug out of the rubble and eased down to the waiting medical teams. All were badly injured and burned. The serious nature of their injuries meant that two were quickly transferred to the famous McIndoe Burns Unit at East Grinstead in Sussex.

Fortunately, like all who have served in the British fire service, it helped that I have first-hand understanding and experience of the way the Fund operates at local level, particularly when a major tragedy strikes.

> *...representatives of the Fund had sprung into action and the mechanism to begin providing immediate financial help, support and assistance to the bereaved families was already in motion.*

Tragically, when the rescue teams finally got to the last trapped fireman, it was too late; he was dead. This fourth member of the buried crew had been one of my young probationers. Earlier, during the first frantic minutes of the fire, he had been one of those who had carried out heroic rescues of residents trapped on ledges high above the spreading fire. Now in the first light of an icy London dawn, we all mourned the loss of this young firefighter.

All four firefighters were married men with children. Three lived outside the Greater London area, yet within an hour, various representatives of the Fund had sprung into action and the mechanism to begin providing immediate financial help, support and assistance to the bereaved families was already in motion. As is so often the case with serious fires involving firefighter fatalities, the Fund's involvement with this particular fire was set to continue for many years to come.

From a personal viewpoint, the Worsley Hotel fire also brought into perspective the value of several highly successful fund-raising events that had been staged at Paddington Fire Station during the previous summer. One particular Open Day saw a large crowd from the local community enjoying the sunshine as they filled the drill yard, flocking around the many stalls, games and activities for adults and children alike. Now,

there were dependants on the station strength who were going to need the help of the Fund for some time to come.

Some of the research material that I have consulted while writing *Out of the Flames* has naturally come from the Fund's own archives at Littlehampton. The historical files of the London Fire Brigade Museum, the Imperial War Museum and the Fire Service College have also been invaluable. But the greatest historical assistance by far was provided by Ronnie Greene's own documents, notes, letters, and photographs assembled during his years as General Organizing Secretary of the embryo London Fund from September 1940 right through to his sudden death in office at Marine Court, Littlehampton in 1978. Maureen Greene readily made Ronnie's extensive archives available to me, and as a result, much of the detailed historical background of the FSNBF was easier to trace and understand.

At the beginning of this story it was the firemen and firewomen of the London Fire Service who bore the first fearsome brunt of the enemy bomber attacks. But all too soon after the dark, early days of the London Blitz, death and injuries to firefighters were occurring in other towns and cities in the United Kingdom. During this time, poorly uniformed and equipped firemen nightly stood alone in the streets facing the bombs and the dangers posed by fly-

Opposite: This dramatic photograph was taken in 1973 soon after the first firefighting crew arrived at a smoke-filled shop in Sunderland. The firemen have pitched a ladder into the first floor and, while returning to the fire engine to pull off a hosereel, the entire shop front has exploded in a flashover. Note that the intense radiated heat has already set fire to the front of the appliance. (Sunderland Fire Brigade)

175

176

ing shrapnel, falling buildings, fire and thick smoke. Today's firefighter also regularly faces levels of danger and hazardous situations that few other people have to confront in time of peace, but modern fire crews are much better trained and prepared for their battle with the age-old enemy, uncontrolled fire.

Another aspect of this story of 60 years of firefighting during peace and war that stands out are the many examples of the sheer resilience and fortitude of the human spirit. This is repeatedly illustrated by examples of the Fund's work with the men, women and children of the British Fire Service, often at a time of personal loss and tragedy.

I only met Ronnie Greene twice during my own career. However, as I have worked steadily through all his many boxes and files spanning over 35 years of the Fund's work, I have grown quite accustomed to his direct, no-nonsense personal style, which is particularly noticeable in papers penned during the early days of the London Blitz. The fact that, as a senior operational officer, he was able to organize and oversee the fast-growing work of the London Fund during those unrelenting days and nights, even before the additional responsibility of the National Fund and its larger structure was shouldered in 1943, is a tribute to the personal stamina, dogged determination and strong beliefs of this very remarkable man.

Indeed, in a number of references made during those dramatic wartime years Ronnie says in correspondence:

"…But you must understand that in the fire service we are all pretty busy people at this time."

Surely none of us can even begin to understand just what an understatement this was.

Now at the end of my task, I am mindful that in addition to all those individually named, either in various passages of *Out of the Flames* or in the Acknowledgements section of the book, there are many others who, in various ways at both national and local level, have been part of the growth and development of the FSNBF over 60 years.

Unfortunately, it is quite impossible to mention all these men and women personally. Nor is it possible to name all the thousands of fire station FSNBF representatives and volunteers up and down the country who have been involved in past or present-day fundraising, and who help to keep the enthusiasm for the Fund at local level at such a high pitch.

Out of the Flames is, in part, a tribute to everyone in this small army and to all those who have in some way been part of the story of this magnificent and outstanding charity and its work within the British Fire Service over the past 60 years.

Another aspect of this story of 60 years of firefighting during peace and war that stands out are the many examples of the sheer resilience and fortitude of the human spirit.

APPENDICES

THE STRUCTURE OF THE FIRE SERVICES NATIONAL BENEVOLENT FUND

Opposite: Crews of Tyne and Wear Metropolitan Fire Brigade get to work to attack a deep-seated fire on several levels during the early stages of a serious blaze in commercial premises in Newcastle. (Tyne and Wear Metropolitan Fire Brigade)

A charitable company limited by guarantee. Company No: 4480058 Charity No: 1093387.

Patron: Her Majesty The Queen

Fund Headquarters

Marine Court,
Fitzalan Road,
Littlehampton,
West Sussex,
BN17 5NF
Telephone: 01903 736063
Fax: 01903 731095

Marine Court

Fitzalan Road,
Littlehampton,
West Sussex,
BN17 5NF
Telephone: 01903 736063
Fax: 01903 731095

Harcombe House

Chudleigh,
Devon,
TQ13 2ND
Telephone: 01626 853639
Fax: 01626 853841

Jubilee House

Eamont Park,
Eamont Bridge,
Penrith,
Cumbria,
CA10 2BN
Telephone: 01768 890009
Fax: 01768 891212

In addition to providing convalescence and beneficial rest at Marine Court and Harcombe House, together with therapy, rehabilitation and nursing care at Jubilee House, the FSNBF provides grants to the following groups:

Widows and Widowers
Young Dependants
Young Special Needs
Less Able
Residential Care Homes
Educational

Furthermore, the FSNBF pays for the monitoring and maintenance charges of lifeline units for disabled and elderly persons living in their own homes. Christmas gifts are provided to those in need, and where appropriate, death grants are also awarded.

SOME SIGNIFICANT HISTORICAL EVENTS

Year	Event
1943	Death Grant £15. Orphans' Allowance 4/0d (20p) per week.
1946	Killed on Duty Grant £100.
1951	Swiss TB Scheme introduced.
1953	HM The Queen becomes Patron of the Fund.
1955	Killed on Duty Grant £400. Orphans' Allowance 10/0d (50p) per week.
1958	Orphans' Allowance 12/6d (62½p).
1960	Education Grants to Orphans.
1962	£100 a year Grants to Totally Disabled.
1963	Orphans' Allowance 20/0d (£1) per week to age 16. Special University Grants.
1964	Killed on Duty Death Grant £1,000. Orphans' Holiday Scheme. Widows' Grants 10/0d (50p) per week.
1965	Opening of Marine Court, Littlehampton.
1966	Widows' Grants 20/0d (£1) per week. Apprenticeship Grants £26 per year.
1967	Totally Disabled Grant increased to £150.
1968	Extension to Marine Court. Apprenticeship Grants increased to £50 per annum.
1969	Widows' Grants increased to £90 per annum.
1970	Killed on Duty Death Grant £2,000. Natural Causes Death Grant £250. Orphans' Allowance increased to 25/0d (£1.25p) per week.
1971	Died on Duty Death Grant introduced £1,000.
1972	Education Grant increased to £2 per week.
1973	Orphans' Allowance increased to £1.50 per week. Natural Causes Death Grants £350. £30 Birthday Grant to aged widows introduced.
1975	Grant up to £50 introduced for widows not eligible for Death Grants.

Year	Event
1976	Extension of Orphans' Allowance to age 17. Inclusion of Northern Ireland firefighters.
1977	Help to Widows Grants increased to £120 per annum plus Birthday Grant. Introduction of scheme to help members of the service with handicapped children.
1978	Opening of Munson House for unaccompanied personnel. Increase in Natural Causes Death Grants to £750. Hardship Grant up to £100 for widows not eligible for Death Grants.
1980	Annual fund-raising income exceeded £1 million for the first time.
1981	Purchase of Harcombe House, Chudleigh, Devon.
1986	Hardship Grant on death of former member increased to £250.
1987	First Give-As-You-Earn scheme (forerunner of Covenant/Gift Aid schemes).
1988	Widows' Annual Grant increased to £200.
1990	Opening of Ronnie Greene Wing, Marine Court, Littlehampton.
1993	Golden Jubilee of the Fund. HM The Queen attends Reception at London's Guildhall.
1995	Opening of Jubilee House Therapy Centre, Eamont Park, Penrith, Cumbria.
1998	Blaze Bear introduced as the Fund's national mascot.
2000	Fund organizes first international "trek".
2001	Annual flag day in London breaks all records with a total of £94,000.
2002	Introduction of Monthly Lottery. Inaugural International Firefighters' Day.

CHAIRMEN OF THE FIRE SERVICES NATIONAL BENEVOLENT FUND 1943-2003

Year	Name	Brigade
1943-46	Sir Andrew Murray	Scottish Home Department
1946-49	AH Johnstone	Surrey
1949-51	KN Hoare	Manchester
1951-53	CV Bentley	Bolton
1953-55	LW Johnson	Birmingham
1955-57	HP Heptinsall	Northamptonshire
1957-59	LA Wood, OBE	Bournemouth
1959-61	A Wooder, CBE	Middlesex
1961-63	Lt.Cdr. J Fordham, CBE	Kent
1963-65	DW Bates, OBE	Glamorgan
1965-67	CJ Murden, MBE	Lincolnshire (Kesteven)
1967-69	ER Ashill, OBE	Hampshire
1969-71	AH Warren, OBE	Cheshire
1971-73	AE Bowles, CBE	Lancashire
1973-75	JB Vickery, OBE	Surrey
1975-77	J Milner, CBE	London
1977-79	W Dancey, OBE	West Glamorgan
1979-80	T Lister, CBE, QFSM	West Midlands
1980-81	RJ Knowlton, CBE, QFSM	Strathclyde
1981-82	S Rankin, QFSM	Merseyside
1982-83	K Horan, CBE, QFSM	West Yorkshire

Year	Name	Brigade
1983-84	D McCallum, OBE	Cambridgeshire
1984-85	JJ Killoran, OBE, QFSM	Devon
1985-86	RA Bullers, CBE, QFSM	London
1986-87	PH Wilson, OBE, QFSM	Nottinghamshire
1987-88	TJL Miles	Suffolk
1988-89	R King, OStJ, QFSM	Dyfed
1989-90	JR Watson, CBE, QFSM	Lancashire
1990-91	CB Halliday, QFSM	Strathclyde
1991-92	AR Kennedy, QFSM	London
1992-93	J Ord, JP, OStJ, QFSM	Northumberland
1993-94	IST Adam, OBE, QFSM	Central Scotland
1994-95	G Meldrum, CBE, QFSM	West Midlands
1995-96	DE Kent, JP	Home Office
1996-97	DJ Williams, KStJ, QFSM	South Wales
1997-98	JG Russel, CBE, QFSM	Lancashire
1998-99	JH Herrick, OStJ, QFSM	Lincolnshire
1999-2000	J Craig, OStJ, QFSM	Wiltshire
2000-2001	G Almond, CBE	Greater Manchester
2001-2002	J O'Connor, MBE, JP	London
2002-2003	K MacGillivray	Strathclyde

184

UNITED KINGDOM PUBLIC FIRE BRIGADES HEADQUARTERS ADDRESSES

Avon Fire Brigade
Temple Back
BRISTOL
BS1 6EU

Bedfordshire & Luton Fire & Rescue Service
Southfields Road
Kempston
BEDFORD
MK42 7NR

Buckinghamshire Fire & Rescue Service
Cambridge Street
AYLESBURY
HP20 1BD

Cambridgeshire Fire & Rescue Service
(Including Peterborough Volunteer Fire Brigade)
Hinchingbrooke Cottage
Brampton Road
HUNTINGDON
PE18 8NA

Central Scotland Fire Brigade
Main Street
Maddiston
FALKIRK
FK2 0LG

Cheshire Fire Brigade
WINSFORD
CW7 2FQ

Cleveland Fire Brigade
Endeavour House
Stockton Road
HARTLEPOOL
TS25 5TB

County Durham & Darlington Fire & Rescue Brigade
Framwellgate Moor
DURHAM
DH1 5JR

Cornwall County Fire Brigade
Old County Hall
Station Road
TRURO
TR1 3AY

Cumbria County Fire Service
Station Road
COCKERMOUTH
CA13 9PR

Derbyshire Fire & Rescue Service
The Old Hall
Burton Road
Littleover
DERBY
DE23 6EH

Devon Fire & Rescue Service
Clyst St George
EXETER
EX3 0NW

Dorset Fire & Rescue Service
Colliton Park
DORCHESTER
DT1 1FB

Dumfries & Galloway Fire Brigade
Brooms Road
DUMFRIES
DG1 2DZ

East Sussex County Fire Brigade HQ
24 King Henry's Road
LEWES
East Sussex
BN7 1BZ

Essex County Fire & Rescue Service HQ
Rayleigh Close
Rayleigh Road
HUTTON
Essex
CM13 1AL

Fife Fire & Rescue Service
Strathore Road
Thornton
Kirkcaldy
FIFE
KY1 4DF

Gloucestershire Fire & Rescue Service
Keynsham Road
CHELTENHAM
GL53 7PY

Grampian Fire Brigade
19 North Anderson Drive
ABERDEEN
AB9 2TP

Greater Manchester County Fire Service
146 Bolton Road
Swinton
MANCHESTER
M27 8US

Hampshire Fire & Rescue Service
Leigh Road
EASTLEIGH
Hants
SO50 9SJ

Hereford & Worcester Fire Brigade
Copenhagen Street
WORCESTER
WR1 2HQ

Hertfordshire Fire & Rescue Service
Old London Road
HERTFORD
SG13 7LD

Highlands & Islands Fire Brigade
16 Harbour Road
Longman West
INVERNESS
DG12DZ

Humberside Fire Brigade
Summergroves Way
Hessel High Road
HULL
HU4 7BB

Isle of Wight Fire & Rescue Service
St Nicholas
58 St John's Road
NEWPORT
PO30 1LT

Isles of Scilly Fire Brigade
Administration Centre
The Airport
ST MARY'S
TR21 0NG

Kent Fire Brigade
Tovil
MAIDSTONE
Kent
ME15 6XB

Lancashire Fire & Rescue Service
Garstang Road
Fulwood
PRESTON
PR2 3LH

Leicestershire Fire & Rescue Service
Anstey Frith
Leicester Road
Glenfield
LEICESTER
LE3 8HD

Lincolnshire Fire Brigade
South Park Avenue
LINCOLN
LN5 8EL

London Fire Brigade
8 Albert Embankment
LONDON
SE1 7SD

Lothian & Borders Fire Brigade
Lauriston Place
EDINBURGH
EH3 9DE

Merseyside Fire Service
Hatton Garden
LIVERPOOL
L3 2AD

Mid & West Wales Fire Brigade
'Ucheldir'
College Road
CARMARTHEN
Dyfed
SA31 3EF

Norfolk Fire Service
Whitegates
Heathersett
NORWICH
NR9 3DN

North Wales Fire Brigade
Llanberis Road
CAERNARFON
Gwynedd
LL55 2DF

North Yorkshire Fire & Rescue Service
Crosby Road
NORTHALLERTON
DL6 1AB

Northamptonshire Fire & Rescue Service
Moulton Way
Moulton Park
NORTHAMPTON
NN3 6SJ

Northern Ireland Fire Brigade
1 Seymour Street
LISBURN
Co Antrim
BT27 4SX

Northumberland Fire & Rescue Service
Loansdean
MORPETH
NE61 2ED

Nottinghamshire Fire & Rescue Service
Bestwood Lodge
Arnold
NOTTINGHAM
NG5 8PD

186

Oxfordshire Fire Service
Sterling Road
Kidlington
OXFORD
OX5 2DU

Royal Berkshire Fire & Rescue Service
103 Dee Road
Tilehurst
READING
RG30 4FS

Shropshire Fire & Rescue Service
St Michael's Street
SHREWSBURY
Shropshire
SY1 2HJ

Somerset Fire Brigade
Hestercombe House
Cheddon Fitzpaine
TAUNTON
TA2 8LQ

South Wales Fire Service
Lanelay Hall
PONTYCLUN
Mid Glamorgan
CF7 9XA

South Yorkshire Fire & Rescue Service
Command HQ
Wellington Street
SHEFFIELD
S1 3FG

Staffordshire Fire & Rescue Service
Pirehill House
STONE
Staffordshire
ST15 0BS

Strathclyde Fire Brigade
Bothwell Road
HAMILTON
Lanarkshire
ML3 0EA

Suffolk County Fire Service
Colchester Road
IPSWICH
Suffolk
IP4 4SS

Surrey Fire & Rescue Service
St David's
70 Wray Park Road
REIGATE
RH2 0EJ

Tayside Fire Brigade
Blackness Road
DUNDEE
DD1 5PA

Tyne & Wear Metropolitan Fire Brigade
Pilgrim Street
NEWCASTLE UPON TYNE
Tyne & Wear
NE99 1HR

Warwickshire Fire & Rescue Service
Warwick Street
LEAMINGTON SPA
CV32 5LH

West Midlands Fire Service
Lancaster Circus
Queensway
BIRMINGHAM
B4 7DE

West Sussex Fire Brigade
Northgate
CHICHESTER
West Sussex
PO19 1BD

West Yorkshire Fire Service
Oakroyd Hall
BIRKENSHAW
West Yorkshire
BD11 2DY

Wiltshire Fire Brigade
Manor House
Potterne
DEVIZES
SN10 5PP

IN ADDITION:

Isle of Man Fire & Rescue Service
Elm Tree House
Onchan
ISLE OF MAN
IM3 4EF

Guernsey Fire Brigade
Town Arsenal
St Peter Port
GUERNSEY
GY1 1UW

Jersey Fire Service
Rouge Bouillon
St Helier
JERSEY
JE2 3ZA

ACKNOWLEDGEMENTS

MANY PEOPLE have been of assistance to me during the research and writing of *Out of the Flames* and their help has been much appreciated.

In particular, Maureen Greene readily allowed me access to all of Ronnie's considerable collection of notes, correspondence, documents and photographs covering some four decades and more, some dating back to the time when the London Fire Service Benevolent Fund was formed in 1940. Maureen was also helpful in clarifying a number of historical points along the way.

Others who deserve my special thanks are: the library staff of the London Fire Brigade Museum, Southwark; the Fire Service College Library, Moreton-in-Marsh; and the Imperial War Museum, London.

Mrs Sandra Bermingham; Sir Graham Meldrum, HM Chief Inspector of Fire Services; DCFO Alan House, Hampshire Fire & Rescue Service; Bob Fitz, retired Chief of Lebanon Fire Department, New Hampshire, USA; Firemaster Jeff Ord, Strathclyde Fire Brigade; Divisional Officer Craig Cook, ADO Billie Milne and various other officers of Strathclyde Fire Brigade; Former Divisional Officer Ken Reed, Royal Berkshire Fire Brigade; Brian Saville and Andrew Hanson, West Yorkshire Fire Service; Edward Ockenden, West Midlands Fire Service; John Chaplin, Editor *Vintage Speedway*; Ken Warner (Maureen Greene's brother); and Leading Firefighter Matt Smith, Oxfordshire Fire Service.

I also appreciate the co-operation of those dependants of the Fund who are mentioned in *Out of the Flames*.

Toni Denyer and Annette Hudders at FSNBF Headquarters at Littlehampton, Carol Tilley, the Fund's East Midland representative, and Barbara D'avino, the Fund's London-based fundraiser, have all been very enthusiastic and helpful throughout the preparation of *Out of the Flames*.

I also wish to thank various Chief Fire Officers and their staff for allowing the publication of a number of brigade photographs and for providing information on particular fires. During my research, it was also useful to draw upon documents and papers from the former Chief Fire Officer of the London Fire Brigade, Sir Freddy Delve, and wartime LFB Senior Staff Officer Arthur Sullivan.

Paul Turner and Sue Pressley of Stonecastle Graphics, the designers of *Out of the Flames*, have done a superb job and deserve my special thanks for the consistently high standard of their work.

Finally, a sincere thank you is due to my wife Susie, who has generally assisted me and kept me both organized and sane throughout the project in her usual quiet and highly efficient manner.

Neil Wallington

FURTHER READING

Blackstone, G.V. *A History of the British Fire Service* (Routledge & Kegan Paul, 1957; new edition Fire Protection Association, 1996)

Collier, Richard. *The City That Wouldn't Die* (Collins, 1959)

Demarne, Cyril. *Our Girls* (Pentland Press, 1995)

Fire & Water – The London Firefighter's Blitz 1940-42 Remembered (Lindsay Drummond, 1942; new edition Firestorm Publications, 1992)

Holloway, Sally. *London's Noble Fire Brigades* (Cassell, 1973)

Holloway, Sally. *Courage High* (HMSO, 1992)

Holloway, Sally/Wallington, Neil. *Fire & Rescue* (Patrick Stephens, 1994)

Honeycombe, Gordon. *Red Watch* (Hutchinson, 1976; Arrow, 1977; new edition Firestorm Publications, 1993)

Jackson. W. Eric. *London's Fire Brigades* (Longmans, 1966)

Nicholls, Arthur. *Going To Blazes* (Hale, 1978)

Waller, Jane/Vaughan-Rees, Michael. *Blitz – The Civilian War* (Macdonald/Optima, 1990)

Wallington, Neil. *Fireman! A Personal Account* (David & Charles, 1979)

Wallington, Neil. *Firemen at War* (David & Charles, 1981)

Wallington, Neil. *999* (David & Charles, 1987)

Wallington, Neil. *Images of Fire* (David & Charles, 1989)

Wallington, Neil. *Firefighter!* (Firestorm Publications, 1992)

Wallington, Neil. *Firefighting – A Pictorial History* (Parragon, 1997)

Wallington, Neil. *Great Fires of London* (Sutton Publishing, 2001)

Wassey, Michael. *Ordeal by Fire* (Secker & Warburg, 1941)

Weightman, Gavin. *Rescue* (Boxtree, 1996)

INDEX

189

192